THE MAKING OF A RACIST

THE MAKING OF A RACIST

A SOUTHERNER
REFLECTS *on*
FAMILY, HISTORY,
and the SLAVE TRADE

CHARLES B. DEW

University of Virginia Press

CHARLOTTESVILLE AND LONDON

University of Virginia Press
© 2016 by the Rector and Visitors of the University of Virginia
All rights reserved
Printed in the United States of America on acid-free paper

First published 2016
First paperback edition published 2017
ISBN 978-0-8139-4039-7 (paper)

9 8 7 6 5 4 3 2

The Library of Congress has cataloged the hardcover edition as follows:
Library of Congress Cataloging-in-Publication Data

Names: Dew, Charles B.
Title: The making of a racist : a southerner reflects on family, history, and the
    slave trade / Charles B. Dew.
Description: Charlottesville : University of Virginia Press, 2016. | Includes
    bibliographical references and index.
Identifiers: LCCN 2015043815 | ISBN 9780813938875 (cloth : acid-free paper) |
    ISBN 9780813938882 (e-book)
Subjects: LCSH: Dew, Charles B. | Dew, Charles B.—Family. | Historians—
    Southern States—Biography. | Southern States—Biography. | Southern
    States—Historiography. | Slavery—Southern States—History. | Slave
    trade—Southern States—History. | Racism—Southern States—History.
    | Southern States—Race relations—History.
Classification: LCC E175.5.D49 A3 2016 | DDC 306.3/620975—dc23
LC record available at http://lccn.loc.gov/2015043815

In memory of
Illinois Browning Culver

CONTENTS

PREFACE

I have been doing my best to make sense of southern history for as long as I can remember. Trying to understand my native region has been the central preoccupation of my intellectual life almost since I learned to read, and, even before that, the South and race were presented to me in the stories my mother read to me, as I describe at the beginning of chapter 2.

I have been teaching southern history now for more than fifty years, and in my classes I have found myself returning over and over again to stories from my childhood and early adulthood as I try to describe to my students how I was raised and how the process of my upbringing imparted the views and beliefs that constitute the core of the first two chapters of this book: my Confederate youth, and the emerging attitudes and beliefs that made me—there is no other way to say this—a racist, an accidental racist perhaps, as my friend the novelist Anne Tyler might put it, but a racist nonetheless.

My students remember these stories. Because they are personal and because they are hearing them from someone who lived it, these scenes from my youth seem to resonate with them; they invariably ask probing questions in class and often stop by my office to continue our discussions. So I decided to write it down. It was not easy. But I found that once I got started, the material began to flow, my memory kicked into gear, and I would often be at my desk for hours on end. I remembered things and events and scenes and conversations I had not thought about for many years. It was almost as if I needed to get this story out.

The result is a strange combination of autobiography and

history—the story of my growing up on the white side of the color line in the Jim Crow South, my engagement as an adult with southern history, and the power of the past, and on occasion a single piece of documentary evidence, to rock us back on our heels and send us off in a quest for understanding. In my case, as I describe in chapter 4, one document, a printed broadside generated by the Richmond, Virginia, slave trade, was just such a piece of historical evidence. It sent me to the archives on a dismal journey: to read as many of the surviving letters of Richmond's slave traders, their agents, and their customers as I could get my hands on.

While I was engaged in researching and writing this book, a scholarly outpouring of remarkable depth and breadth focusing on the domestic slave trade in the United States occurred. This began with Maurie D. McInnis's brilliant *Slaves Waiting for Sale: Abolitionist Art and the American Slave Trade,* which appeared in 2011. Her book was followed in rapid succession by four equally impressive studies: Walter Johnson's *River of Dark Dreams: Slavery and Empire in the Cotton Kingdom,* published in 2013; Sven Beckert's *Empire of Cotton: A Global History* and Edward E. Baptist's *The Half Has Never Been Told: Slavery and the Making of American Capitalism,* both published in 2014; and Calvin Schermerhorn's *The Business of Slavery and the Rise of American Capitalism, 1815–1860,* which appeared in 2015.

Maurie McInnis proved herself as adept at slave history as she was at art history, and the result was the most accurate and detailed portrait we have ever had of the Richmond slave-trading community, its personnel, its physical setting, and the art that came into being as observers turned their attention to the scenes that unfolded in slave traders' auction rooms. The Johnson, Beckert, Baptist, and Schermerhorn studies all drive home a point of transcendent importance: this traffic was absolutely vital for the antebellum rise of the Cotton Kingdom in the Deep South, and in the course of filling the Lower South's voracious demand for labor, the basic contours of American capitalism took shape in the nineteenth century.

All five of these studies deserve the widest possible readership; anyone who does this will be stunned by the extraordinary research, the deft writing, and the impressive interpretative analysis that went into each of these volumes. I learned an enormous amount from them. But, in the end, I decided not to add a discussion of this scholarship to this undertaking. Certainly the material I present in the second half of this book—the letters of the Richmond slave trade—confirms the thrust of this new scholarship, but I read these letters with a different purpose in mind: I was trying to get inside the minds of the white participants in the city's human trafficking to see if I could come to grips with how my people—southerners—could engage in this abhorrent business and not see the evil inherent in what they were doing. But the documentary evidence I have presented about the Richmond slave trade certainly complements this new scholarship, giving, I hope, added depth to the story told in these five extremely impressive volumes.

So, to repeat, I have written a strange hybrid, a combination of autobiography and history that does not fit neatly into any category of writing with which I am familiar, something my father would have called "a different breed of cat." But I hope what I have written down here will resonate with at least some readers in ways that parallel the reaction of many of my students over the years: something remembered that helps them understand how the South of our day came into being, something that helps explain the racism that for far too long has poisoned the atmosphere of the place where I was born and raised. If I manage to bring some readers along with me on this journey, I will have accomplished what I set out to do.

CHARLES B. DEW
WILLIAMSTOWN, MASS.

THE MAKING OF A RACIST

Introduction

THE STUFF OF HISTORY

I love to teach from original documents, and my favorites tend to be those I turned up myself during archival searches. There is something special about the contact we make with the past by touching the stuff of history—the letters, the diaries, the record books, the broadsides, and other original materials that pass through our hands as we sit in those quiet and frequently beautiful manuscript reading rooms. We open a folder or a bound manuscript volume or pick up a printed broadside, and we suddenly discover something that changes how we view the history of a subject we are trying to unravel. On rare occasions, we find a document that alters how we feel about ourselves and what we are doing with our lives.

This is a book inspired by just such documents, and one document in particular. It has its origin in items I have found over the years that forced me to stop dead in my tracks and lay my pencil down on the table in front of me as I tried to come to grips with what I had just read.

Always, and particularly in these moments, I have been trying to understand the American South, the region of the country where I was born and raised. Often my geographic focal point turned out to be Virginia. My ancestors came from there, and one of them, Thomas Roderick Dew, offered up an observation that will figure largely in subsequent chapters of this book. "Virginia is in fact a *negro* raising state," he wrote in 1832; "she produces enough for her own supply and six thousand for sale."[1]

Mentioning Thomas Roderick Dew brings me to a second point I want to make about the stuff of history. Our individual lives fall under that heading as well. Historians do not spring full-blown from the head of Zeus. We come from families, both in an immediate and a historic sense. We get where we end up as historians through a process, through our own experience, through life as we have lived it—when and where we were born, our mothers and fathers, our siblings, our extended families, who our forebearers were, the culture in which we grew up, how we were raised, where we went to school, what we learned, the times in which we live, all of this and much, much more goes into making us decide to spend our lives studying the past and trying to pass the results of our quest for understanding on to our students. It is a highly personal business, this business of studying history. It takes a trigger, often a great teacher, to transform our curiosity about the past into a passion. And it does take passion, make no mistake—a passionate desire to know, to comprehend, to understand. It is the joining of these two strands of the stuff of history, the scholarly and the personal, that this book is all about.

I know that I am cutting against the grain of my profession here. History disembodied from the historian has a long and rich tradition in this country. It is what I was taught in graduate school. We should try to be scientists, we were told, albeit "social scientists." Strip the personal out of our scholarship. We had two questions to ask, I recall one of my graduate school professors telling me: what's the story I want to tell and what does it all mean? This was good advice in many ways, but I have decided at this point in my life—not quite made it to four score years but almost there—that I want to put some of the personal back into history, or at least the history that I try to write. So that too is what this book is about.

1

A Confederate Youth

I came by my Confederate youth naturally. I was born in the South, my parents were both southerners, ancestors on both sides fought for the Confederacy, and one of my antebellum forebearers probably did as much as anyone in his time to make the defense of slavery an intellectually legitimate exercise. But one must still be taught. A description of that process—my education as a Confederate youth—seems the best way to start this story.

To begin at the very beginning, I was born in 1937 in St. Petersburg, Florida. My mother, Amy Meek Dew, and my father, Jack Carlos Dew, were both, to repeat, dyed-in-the-wool southerners, although my mother's place of birth, Wayne County, West Virginia, might not suggest that at first glance.

My father's roots were unmistakably southern—Tennessee— but as it happened, he was born in 1903 in Lake Charles, Louisiana. His father, my grandfather, Charles Givens Dew, made his living farming and digging water wells in and around the town of Trenton in West Tennessee, and he had taken his drilling equipment to Louisiana in hopes of striking oil. As it turned out, he was drilling in the right place but ran out of pipe before he hit the precious stuff, or at least that was what I was told growing up. No one had the good sense to lend him money for more pipe, thus depriving the Dew clan of what my boyhood imagination saw as a mighty gusher of black gold.[1]

Grandfather Givens, as he was known in the family, went back to Tennessee with a new son in the family but not much else. He also brought with him a fatal disease. Somewhere along the way, he had managed to contract tuberculosis, and it was this circumstance that led the family to the West Coast of Florida.

Local boosters touted the supposedly salubrious climate around St. Petersburg as a cure for just about any malady known to mankind, and this was where the family settled in 1912.[2] Four years later, my grandfather died at the age of fifty, leaving a widow and six children—three boys and three girls. My father was thirteen at the time his father died. One of the girls, my aunt Maude, remembered visiting her father in the sanatorium separated from him by a glass window to prevent physical contact and the possible spread of infection.

My father was the youngest of the three boys in the family, and they worked hard in the following years to support their mother and their three sisters. It was not an easy life for any of them. The two older boys, Roy and Joe, clerked in a local hardware store, and my father rose before dawn to sell newspapers to the drummers who arrived in downtown St. Petersburg on the early morning trains. But those three boys remained persistent, using their considerable drive and intelligence to begin a process that culminated in their eventual emergence as leading citizens of St. Pete, as everyone called my hometown.

Hardware stores in those early twentieth-century days sold an amazing array of merchandise, everything from the usual tools and building supplies to furniture and automobiles. These last two items turned out to be the keys to my family's rise to local prominence. Roy focused on car sales and Joe on furniture, eventually working his way up to manager of the furniture department. The storeowners, apparently raised in the marrow of nineteenth-century hardware store tradition, were not all that interested in selling automobiles or furniture, so the two Dew boys made their move. As my father told the story, Roy managed to borrow the money to buy the Ford, Buick, and Cadillac franchises. Joe, with what he had learned in the furniture trade, managed to acquire a partner and open his own store. Both men thrived. Roy sold the Ford and half the Buick franchises to pay off his creditors; the Cadillac franchise he wisely kept for himself. Joe's furniture business rose on the crest of the Florida boom in the early 1920s and soon became one of the leading stores in the area.

In subsequent years, I never had to explain locally that my name was "Dew" and not "Drew." My uncles' two businesses, Dew Cadillac and Dew Furniture, were household names in St. Pete. The Dew Motor Company was housed in a handsome white stucco building a few blocks south of Central Avenue, the main business thoroughfare. The Dew Furniture Company occupied several upper floors of Wilson-Chase & Company, the leading department store in town. Uncle Roy sold those huge Cadillacs to the rising money class of local businessmen and made a small fortune in the process. Uncle Joe may not have invented the term "loss leaders," but he certainly knew how to get customers into his store. His sales were trumpeted by outsized ads in the local papers, and Uncle Joe eventually moved to a fine house at nearby Pass-A-Grille Beach and ended up as the commodore of the Pass-A-Grille Yacht Club. Not bad for a couple of small-town southern boys who never got past high school.

When my father finished his high school education—at St. Pete High—his two older brothers paid for both his undergraduate and law school education at the University of Virginia. Jack Dew thus became the first member of his immediate family to go to college. He loved UVa, joined a fraternity, and ended up earning his law degree in 1926. Upon graduation, he took a position with one of the leading law firms in St. Petersburg.

I never really thought of my family as characters out of a Faulkner novel, but looking back on it, I may have missed something there. We clearly were not Sartorises, the Mississippi planter-aristocrats who stood at the top of Faulkner's fictional food chain. But I certainly did not think of us as Snopeses, either—no one was named "Montgomery Ward" Dew or "Wall Street Panic" Dew or "Admiral Dewey" Dew or even "Flem" Dew (although I did have an Uncle Flip, married to my father's middle sister, Doris, and a great favorite of mine growing up).

There was, nevertheless, something at least mildly Faulknerian about the rise of the Dew family. Uncle Roy was capable of some fascinating turns on the English language, and Uncle Joe's pencil moustache and swarthy complexion (a heritage of some Spanish ancestry in our family tree, as was my father's middle name, Carlos) made him something of an exotic character in my youthful eyes. But whatever their rags-to-riches southern story might entail, I was intensely proud of my family. And I was intensely proud of my father as well. I can still recall the day one of my Sunday school teachers, a young, well-spoken stockbroker newly arrived in town, referred to him as "the best lawyer in St. Petersburg." The family of a peripatetic well digger from West Tennessee had come a long way.

My father's time at the University of Virginia turned out to be fortunate in more ways than one. In addition to receiving a first-rate education during his years there, he also encountered a rather shy and quite lovely young woman by the name of Amy Kirk Meek. Her brother Jack Meek was a law school classmate of my father's, and it was through him that my father and mother first met. Amy Meek was the daughter of a well-established family in Huntington, West Virginia—her father was a prominent attorney, and her mother, Charlie (yes, Charlie) Burgess Meek, came from a nearby Wayne County family of impeccable southern roots. My mother grew up with two brothers who watched over her like a hawk until she finally went away to boarding school, first Foxcroft in Virginia and then Holton Arms in Washington, DC.

If my father's family had a hint of the Snopeses in their back-

My father, Jack Carlos Dew, in a portrait photograph taken
about the time of his marriage to my mother.

ground, my mother definitely had an element of the Sartorises in
hers. But that difference, as far as I could tell, was never a problem for either one of them. They certainly made a very handsome
couple; the photographs from those days are clear evidence of that.
After several years of courtship while my father was trying to build
up a law practice, they set a date for their wedding.

Their marriage plans were rudely interrupted by the onset of
the Great Depression. As my father told the story, he had managed
to save up enough money to take his new bride on a honeymoon
and was standing in line outside the Central National Bank in St.
Petersburg when the bank closed its doors—for good. His savings
went up in smoke, and it took him a full year to save enough to set
their plans in motion again.

Finally, on a blistering hot West Virginia day in the summer of
1931, their wedding took place. It was an elaborate affair, I remember my mother saying, held in the side yard of the Meeks' hand-

My mother, Amy Meek Dew. This is her wedding portrait,
taken in Huntington, West Virginia, in 1931.

some brick residence in Huntington. Her wedding portrait shows
a lovely, smiling young woman in a beautiful white satin dress, her
face framed by a floral lace garland, holding what appears to be a
white prayer book. The word "radiant" is overused in this context,
but that is how she has always looked to me in this photograph,
even when I was too young to know what the word meant.

Following the ceremony, the newly married couple journeyed
up into the mountains to the famous Greenbrier hotel for their
honeymoon. My father had managed to save up enough to cover
their stay. I still have on my dresser at home a large, silver-colored
shoehorn stamped on the back "The Greenbrier & Cottages
White Sulphur Springs, W.Va.," a keepsake one of them brought
home to mark the occasion.

Dear, my brother, John, and me.
This studio portrait was taken in 1937.

The marriage of Jack Carlos Dew, twenty-eight, and Amy Kirk
Meek, twenty-six, on June 27, 1931, would last a lifetime for both.
There was never a doubt in my mind as I was growing up that the
two of them loved and respected each other deeply. Despite some
tough times that lay ahead, I never heard either one of them say
anything disparaging about the other.

They took up residence in St. Petersburg, and my father began
establishing his law practice. My brother was the first child to arrive. John Carlos Dew was born in 1934, and I came along almost
exactly three years later. That same year, 1937, we moved into a
two-story white frame house on the north side—the better side—
of St. Petersburg. That comfortable house, at 234 Twenty-Fifth
Avenue North, would be my home for the next twenty-one years.

My father eventually made enough for us to move to a tonier neighborhood, but he was never interested in doing so. Indeed, I think he took some satisfaction in refusing to join those other lawyers over on Snell Isle and Brightwaters Boulevard. The place in which he lived suited him just fine, and there was no need to "put on the dog," as he would say, by spending the money for a waterfront view.

My mother's hand provided the soft touch in our household. Amy Meek Dew was a lovely person. There is no other way to describe her. She was attractive, certainly, and nothing short of beautiful in my eyes, but it was her gentle, caring nature that everyone noticed as soon as they came into contact with her. It had an almost luminous quality about it. Even her name in the family reflected the innate kindness that lay at the core of her being; my brother and I called her "Dear." This came about before I was born when she and John were visiting her family in Huntington. Someone, I am not sure who, tried to get my brother to call her "Mother Dear." It was too much for a toddler, but John did manage to get the "Dear" part out, and it stuck.

Deeply religious, Dear brought my brother and me up within the comfortable confines of the Episcopal faith. She loved the quiet eloquence of the Book of Common Prayer and provided both of us with our own copies as soon as we were reasonably proficient readers. She did not criticize other faiths, but it was clear to us that she did not approve of the Bible-thumping histrionics that characterized services at some of the other Protestant churches in our hometown. Her God was a benevolent God who looked out for all of his earthly children. "The Good Lord" was how she invariably referred to the Almighty.

My mother's gentle nature was complemented by a delightful sense of humor. She had a wonderful laugh, took genuine delight in the vagaries and absurdities of the world, and was especially adept at poking fun at herself. I recall her telling me when I was older that she could not understand why no one ever told a dirty joke around her. It was not that she particularly wanted to hear them; it was just that she did not think of herself as a prude and did not want others to think of her that way, either. But I knew exactly why people did not tell those jokes around her. Her manner and her presence, simply who she was, brought out the best qualities in those around her. You would no more tell an off-color joke around my mother than you would take the Lord's name in vain at the Communion rail.

Our father showed the reserve around his sons that fathers of that era customarily displayed, but I never doubted that he loved my brother and me as well, and that he wanted the best for us. We also knew not to cross him. There was a straight-ahead, no-nonsense quality about him that usually kept us in line without being reminded of how we were supposed to behave. John and I were anything but "goody two-shoes," but we were on our best behavior whenever Pop, as we called him, was around. When he whistled in the late afternoon to call us home for dinner—we played outdoors continuously in the numerous vacant lots in our neighborhood, building forts and occasionally puffing on a cigarette one of our buddies had swiped from home—we dropped whatever it was we were doing and headed for our back porch without hesitation. The sound of Pop's piercing whistle carried for blocks, and it never occurred to us to claim we had not heard it.

I got a dramatic illustration of his "don't mess with me" anger when I was five or six years old. World War II was on, and Pop, who had been too young to serve in World War I, was now too old to serve in the current conflict. He was our neighborhood air raid warden, was issued a World War I–era steel helmet to wear on his rounds, and was taxed with making sure the tree trunks that lined the streets of our neighborhood were painted white up to waist level so they could be seen during blackouts. It was heady stuff for my brother and me, although we did not take so readily to working in the victory garden Pop planted (to mollify us, I suspect, he also erected a fabulous double swing set in our backyard that became a magnet for every child in the neighborhood). It was clear to us that he was doing what he could for the war effort.

Rationing of gasoline and rubber was also on, and Pop rode the municipal bus to work every morning from the corner of Twenty Fifth Avenue and Fourth Street, which was the main route downtown from our part of the city (it was, of course, a segregated bus, with "colored" passengers required by law to move to the rear). To provide a place to sit while he and others waited for the bus, he moved a high-backed wooden bench from our breakfast nook at home up to the corner so that the hot, muggy weather that settled in early in the day would not wilt him (in his business suit, snap-brim hat, and freshly shined spectator shoes) before he even got to his office.

The bench lasted one day on the corner. Its disappearance produced a cold fury in Pop and an immediate neighborhood-wide search for the missing item. We did not have to look far. Connie (short for Constantine) and Socs (short for Socrates) Trangus, who owned the popular Oceanana Restaurant at the corner of Fourth Street and Twenty-Fourth Avenue, had spotted the bench and apparently decided it would look good in front of their establishment. And there it sat.

This news created an immediate sense of unease for me. I considered Socs Trangus something of a pal. Connie was the front man who took care of the customers and Socs was the cook. I sat on a high wooden stool in his kitchen on a fairly regular basis, watching him at work in front of the massive black ranges that seemed to fill the kitchen at the rear of the Oceanana. With instructions to hold the china platter tightly in both hands, I was sent the half block up the alley behind our house to the restaurant to pick up dinner for all of us when Dear wanted a break from cooking, which happened fairly often in the late afternoon in our unair-conditioned home. I would take my place on the stool and wait for Socs to fill our order—fried shrimp or scallops, French-fried potatoes, coleslaw, and, my favorite, hamburger steak smothered in rich brown gravy. Socs did not say a lot on these occasions, but he did not treat me like a kid who didn't know anything, either. We were both there just doing our jobs.

So it was with some trepidation that I witnessed, and participated in, the events that unfolded after the discovery of that missing bench. Pop mobilized my brother and me and just about every other boy in the neighborhood, took the removable wooden sides off John's Radio Flyer wagon, and off we headed for the Oceanana, with Pop leading the way. I don't know what he said to Connie and Socs; he went into the restaurant while we stayed outside. But I remember the look of determination on his face when he came out, and I remember loading the bench onto John's wagon and steadying it with many young hands as we rolled it back to the corner. It remained there for the duration of the war, a symbol, in my youthful eyes, of my father's prowess and his willingness to take immediate action to right a wrong. Fortunately, Socs did not seem offended by all of this. My subsequent visits to the Oceanana were no different from those that had gone before. We two just continued to do our jobs.

Pop's sense of right and wrong was much more of a secular than a religious matter. As a boy, he had been a regular attendee at the Presbyterian Church Sunday school, earning medals for not missing a single class, year after year. But as my mother told the story, his experience as a young teenager selling newspapers at the crack of dawn had changed his ideas about organized religion. He had seen church fathers returning from late-night visits to the Negro section of town, and he was old enough to know what they had been up to. Their hypocrisy stuck in his craw and solidified into a hostility toward formal religion that lasted for the rest of his life.

Dear made sure that John and I attended church regularly, but she had the good sense not to try to argue Pop out of his convictions. He was generally sitting in his favorite rocking chair reading the Sunday paper when we left for church, and he was often still there when we came home. He never raised the topic of religion, but if it did happen to come up, he would promptly close the conversation by dismissing the entire subject as "a bunch of who shot John."

Pop's disdain for pretension, and stuffed shirts in general, was displayed in other ways as well. He had no time for civic clubs, for example, even though a membership in one like the Rotary Club would certainly have been good for business. In a large, well-stuffed bookcase that sat next to his rocking chair in the "sunroom," as we called the sitting room at the rear of the house where we all gathered in the evening (the big Philco radio was there), he kept a well-worn copy of a back issue of H. L. Mencken's *American Mercury* magazine. Pop wanted it within easy reach because it contained a short story entitled—I remember exactly—"A Pretty Cute Little Trick." This brief tale was a withering satire of civic clubs and their members who had been taken in by a clever grifter using a religious con. When I became old enough to read, Pop enjoyed no end having me read it out loud, and I loved doing so, because his laughter would fill the house on these occasions.

Pop's idiosyncrasies were pretty much benign, but one of them was downright dangerous: he was a hellhound behind the wheel. My father was a superb driver when it came to the mechanics, but he could not stand to be behind anyone, and I mean anyone, on the road. If we were going anywhere that required us to get out on the highway (to visit aunts and uncles in Clearwater or Lakeland, for example, which we did frequently), he would gun our black 1939 Buick four-door sedan as soon as we hit open pavement and drive like he was one of Joie Chitwood's Auto Daredevils. We would zoom by everything, challenging curves to delay their bend until we blasted past whatever it was in front of us. Defensive driver he was not, and the risk to life and limb was that much greater in that pre–seat belt, pre-airbag era. But we all survived, and, as far as I know, Pop never had a serious accident. Someone looking for evidence of divine intercession in the affairs of man could do worse than point to my father's safe driving record as proof of the existence of a compassionate Higher Power. His advice to me when I was fourteen and he was teaching me how to drive reached the height of irony: "Son, drive like everyone else on the road is a goddamned fool."

As I went through public schools in St. Petersburg—North Ward Elementary and then Mirror Lake Junior High—I gradually became aware that something called history had happened to my people and my part of the world. To put it simply, I was growing into a Confederate youth. My cultural moorings on both sides of my family were unmistakably southern, but it was my father's mother, Bessie Lane Dew, who was the source of much of my early education in these matters (my maternal grandmother, Charlie Burgess Meek, had died in an automobile accident when I was an infant). Grandmother Dew lived in St. Petersburg, where she was an active member of the United Daughters of the Confederacy. Whenever I went to visit her, which I did frequently, she made sure that I spent some time with the *United Daughters of the Confederacy Magazine,* copies of which were always prominently laid out on a coffee table in her living room. When I grew a little older, she gave me my own subscription to the *UDC Magazine.* And it was she who first told me that my father's first name was Jack, not John, because of my Grandfather Givens's reverence for Stonewall Jackson. Pop jokingly remarked that being named Jack had caused no end of confusion over the years, so when it came time to name my older brother, he and Dear settled on John without hesitation.

My sense of history came fully into focus in 1951 on my fourteenth birthday, when my father presented me with twin gifts that marked my coming of age as a white son of the South: a .22-caliber

Marlin bolt-action rifle and Douglas Southall Freeman's massive three-volume history of the Army of Northern Virginia, *Lee's Lieutenants*.[3] It was a challenge for a fourteen-year-old to take on Freeman's magisterial and imposing history of Robert E. Lee's famous army, but I managed to work my way through all three volumes during the course of that year (it helped that my birthday occurred during the first week of January, normally a source of some irritation to me coming so close to Christmas). My .22 went with me everywhere I could possibly take it. It was not a Civil War musket, of course, but it certainly was one in my imagination. I never enjoyed hunting—killing a defenseless animal never made any sense or appealed to me. But I loved to shoot—paper bull's-eye targets, cans, bottles, anything would do. Invariably, the inanimate objects at which I took aim would suddenly become forms on a battlefield—Manassas, Sharpsburg, Gettysburg, Cold Harbor— moving into my line of fire, hostile, menacing, and always clad in blue. Dreaming of Civil War battles constituted a major element of my southern boyhood, and the casualties I was able to inflict with my trusty .22 were staggering.

Fourteen turned out to be a big year for me when it came to reading matter. U. C. Barrett (very few people knew what those initials stood for, but for some reason I did—Uel Curtis), one of my father's partners in the firm of Cook, Harris, Barrett, Mc-Glothlin & Dew, gave me a slender volume entitled *Facts the Historians Leave Out: A Youth's Confederate Primer*. The author's name and qualifications, as they were printed on the title page, were "John S. Tilley, M.A. (Harvard)," the publication date was that same year, 1951, and the book was dedicated "To the Memory of John M. Tilley, Officer in Confederate Army Killed in Action." Additional copies could be purchased for $1.50 postpaid by sending that sum to the author's address in Montgomery, Alabama, with the instructions to "please print name and address plainly." I never felt the need to order any more copies back then. All I needed to know was already in hand. In any case, my immediate patronage was not needed; when I tracked down a copy online in 2014, the edition that arrived at my door was from the seventeenth printing, dated 1971.[4]

Mr. Barrett, as I always called him, was a southern gentleman through and through—white hair, courtly manners, always immaculately dressed, the possessor of a sly wit in near-constant employ, and a Georgia accent as mellifluous as a pool of molasses on a stack of buckwheat cakes (like all southerners, I sometimes get carried away). I am not sure why he passed this book on to me, but I suspect that he, too, felt it was important for a southern boy to grow up on the right side of history.

It was obvious before I even opened it that my *Primer* had a clear and unequivocal message. The cover illustration showed two crossed flags hanging proudly from their staffs: to the left, a Confederate St. Andrew's Cross battle flag; to the right, the last civilian flag of the Confederate States of America. If I were looking for confirmation of my already emerging pro-Confederate biases, I did not have to turn many pages of this small volume to find it.

"Southern men"—Patrick Henry, George Washington, Thomas Jefferson, James Madison—founded "our nation."

The North was basically responsible for slavery. "The Puritans of Massachusetts . . . carried on a large trade in negroes imported from overseas," and by 1787, "Rhode Island held first place in the traffic." But not for long. "New York City forged to the front," and then "Philadelphia soon found the slave-business attractive." And so "what did the Northern traders do with their slaves?" Tilley asked. "They sold them to Southern planters."

Most southern slave owners treated their slaves well, the author claimed, and for good reason: "If he paid $1,000 for a worker would he be so shortsighted as to starve or mistreat him?" And besides, since most slaves were "childlike, good natured, well-behaved" field hands, severe discipline was unnecessary.

On states' rights: "It was only when the Washington Government began reaching out for too much power that the issue of States' Rights became important. States' Rights advocates are loyal to the United States, but they wish to be left alone to manage State affairs."

On "Northern Violation of States' Rights": Abolitionists in the North threatened the South by encouraging slave rebellion—Nat Turner, John Brown's Raid. "Do you wonder that the prospect of slave-uprisings carried terror to every Southern fireside?" Tilley asked. Southerners had no choice but "to form their own government, one which could and would afford protection for their families and homes."

On wartime defeat: "The North had a white population four times as large as that of the South." In addition, "the South had no army, no navy, no treasury, no adequate munitions plants, practically no manufacturing." Given those circumstances, "Only men fighting for what they regarded [as] a lofty principle would have endured the hardships of the Confederate soldier."

On "Reconstruction—A Program of Vengeance": Northerners seeking to punish southerners after the war "were willing to turn the South into a 'graveyard of whites,' a section governed by Negroes 'upheld by Northern white bayonets.'"

Finally, in a chapter entitled "Some Reasons for Secession," the author summarized the lessons southern youth should take away from his *Primer.* Tellingly, he cast this summary in terms of what "A Confederate soldier would likely have told you":

1. Our States entered the Union with the understanding that they had the right to withdraw when membership proved unhappy.
2. We were tired of being gypped by unfair tariff laws.
3. We were fed up with insane abuse from South-hating fanatics.
4. We had bought our slaves from the North, only to learn later that it proposed to free them without a penny of compensation.

5. Northern fanatics had inspired murderous slave-uprisings. Why wait for more?
6. A rabidly-sectional party was in control at Washington.
7. We had no idea of making war. We planned to relieve the North from further association with us.[5]

So there it was. Basically all I needed to know about southern history. My training as a Confederate youth had pretty much been completed when I was in my early teens. I could have stopped at this point and remained warm and content in a cocoon of Dixie myth, angry over what had been done to my land and my people, but secure in my knowledge that history was on our side: we, not the vile Yankees, were the righteous and the aggrieved party in that great, bloody, god-awful, glorious War Between the States.

Later that same year, 1951, I left my native Florida to attend Woodberry Forest, an all-boys independent school in Virginia. As had been the case with my brother, the decision to go away to school was more or less mine to make. St. Pete High, my father's alma mater, had been built early in the twentieth century and was the only high school in our town, which had a population of over 100,000 people by then. Two shifts of students were being run into St. Pete High, one from 7 a.m. until noon, and a second from noon to 5 p.m. As Pop explained it to me, St. Petersburg had become a haven for Yankee retirees, mainly midwesterners, and they steadfastly refused even to consider increasing their property taxes to pay for a second high school. So he left it up to us, first John and then me: stay home and go to St. Pete High, or head off to Virginia and presumably a better education than we could expect to receive at our local school. John chose Woodberry, and off he went when I was eleven years old. As soon as he departed, I gave up my twin bed in what was known as the "baby room" and moved into John's vacated bed on the multiwindowed, and much cooler, sleeping porch at the upstairs rear of our house.

Three years later, it was my turn to decide. Whether to go or to stay home was not an easy decision for me. In addition to inheriting John's more comfortable quarters, I had pretty much been leading an idyllic southern boy's life in St. Pete: literally going barefoot all summer for as long as I could remember, living in a neighborhood filled with kids my own age, riding my bike to school every morning (no school bus for me, despite Dear's misgivings), playing on a six-man football team in a city recreational league, earning a letter in track at Mirror Lake Junior High, reading omnivorously, shooting my .22 (and I had had a BB gun before that), confident of my family's standing in the community, breezing through the public schools with a minimum of effort, getting myself elected to some cushy school positions (King of the May at North Ward and class president at Mirror Lake), and beginning to discover girls in my junior high class. To make going away even less appealing, I had to attend summer school at Woodberry just to get into the regular session beginning in the fall; my entrance exams had been a cold-shower wake-up call on what I had managed not to learn up to that point. Still, there were those double shifts at St. Pete High. I did not like that prospect at all. And it eased the road to Woodberry considerably when I learned that John had been chosen to serve as senior prefect during his sixth-form (i.e., senior) year, the year I would be starting as a fourth-form (i.e., sophomore) new boy.

Woodberry Forest School is a stunningly beautiful place located in the rolling Virginia Piedmont just outside the small town of Orange. The campus of imposing red brick and white-columned buildings was surrounded by green athletic fields, a working farm, and a nine-hole golf course, with a magnificent visual backdrop of the Blue Ridge Mountains in the western distance. While I was a student there, I roamed the nearby Confederate trenches, leaf-filled but still clearly visible, along the south bank of the Rapidan River, where men from Lee's Army of Northern Virginia had wintered in 1864–65. The Confederate battle flag that hung in

Captain of the junior varsity football team at
Woodberry Forest School, fall of 1952.

my dorm room during my three years at Woodberry bore witness
to my love for the South and a near reverence for the soldiers in
gray who had manned those trenches on the Rapidan in defense
of my native region.

In some ways, I did a lot of growing up during my time at
Woodberry. Mandatory evening study halls, supervised by masters (as we referred to our teachers), were a major irritant and were
absolutely vital to my emergence as a decent student who could
aspire to making it into a decent college. We read constantly, even
over the summer (I thought I would never make it through O. E.
Rølvaag's *Giants in the Earth*), we memorized (I can still recite
long passages of "Thanatopsis"), we took tests and exams (all
the time, it seemed to me), we had math and lab science courses
that drove me crazy, and we competed on those green, frequently

muddy, athletic fields all three seasons of every year (football and winter and spring track for me).

At the end of my fifth-form year, I was awarded the Princeton Book Prize, dated June 6, 1953, carrying an inscription that would serve as a source of great amusement in my own family many years later:

"Awarded by the Alumni of Princeton University Living in Orange County, Virginia, to Charles Burgess Dew of Woodberry Forest School for His Outstanding Development in Character and in Academic Achievement."[6]

It is that word "development" that has caused so much delight, particularly when applied to my previous, and presumably deeply flawed, "character." "How low did you start out, Dad?" was the query from my two sons, just before they both started laughing.

One thing I did develop further during my time at Woodberry was my already strong belief that the South had suffered greatly at the hands of the all-too-powerful Yankees during our long decades of sectional competition. My fifth-form American history teacher, Colonel Robert Lee Rogers (aka "Colonel Hoochie"—every master had a nickname), United States Army, Retired, made sure we understood those sad circumstances clearly enough. But, truth be told, I needed no convincing on this point. Everything I had learned growing up pointed in exactly the same direction. From perfectly legal and fully justified secession through four bloody and bitter years of war and defeat and into the dreadful era of Black Reconstruction ("worse than the war," I had been told countless times), the South, my South, the white South, had been on the side of the angels. These were my firm and unyielding convictions; anyone who thought otherwise was either an arrogant, and ignorant, Yankee or certifiably insane. If I did indeed grow in some important ways during these three years in Virginia, in other ways I remained frozen in time. I was, at seventeen, older, certainly, and better educated in a number of respects, but I was still very much a boy of the South, a true son of Dixie, a proud Confederate youth, through and through.

During the spring of my sixth-form year, something momentous happened less than a hundred miles north of Woodberry that went right over my head at the time. It should not have. On May 17, 1954, a unanimous decision of the United States Supreme Court in the case of *Brown v. Board of Education of Topeka* held that racial segregation in public education was unconstitutional, a clear violation of the equal protection of the laws clause of the Fourteenth Amendment. I was too preoccupied with final exams and graduation to realize that the South had just been rocked by a legal, social, and political earthquake, that something revolutionary had happened to my part of the world, something that had the potential to change everything I had grown up believing with regard to race.

I certainly got an earful about *Brown* when I returned home that summer. Pop had held his tongue, out of deference to my mother, I suspect, during graduation, but he felt no such restraint once we all returned to Florida. The *Brown* decision had infuriated him, and he dismissed it as a gross violation of true constitutional principles. My father was an excellent lawyer; I never doubted that for a minute. But his views on politics would have been a better fit for the antebellum South than for what I naively imagined was a much more enlightened twentieth-century South. And his political views certainly bled into his opinion of *Brown*. Chief Justice Earl Warren and the rest of the vindictive cabal he had browbeaten into a unanimous Court were all, to use a dismissive phrase Pop employed often, "not worth the powder to blow them up." This was probably the tamest comment he made on the *Brown* decision.

I had known for years that Pop was, to put it mildly, a rock-ribbed conservative. I am not sure how he came to form his political opinions; I never had the temerity to ask him. He was what the philosopher Eric Hoffer called a "true believer," and I think I knew without being told that true believers just assume they have a lock on the truth. Dear thought two of the senior members of his firm had had a major influence on him from the time he joined their law office. And his views certainly did not reflect his more or less humble roots, first in Tennessee and then in St. Petersburg. But whatever the reasons, Pop was passionate about his conserva tive beliefs. With him, it was my way or the highway, to quote an overused phrase.

My father did not curse all that often around the three of us, but the mere mention of Franklin D. Roosevelt's name would set him off. Had he been religious, he would have considered FDR the anti-Christ. Roosevelt was a "turncoat" who was a "traitor to his class" (which, again, was certainly not the class Pop came from), was clearly a "Communist" and a "Socialist" under that veneer of "Liberalism" (which was, in my father's eyes, pretty much communism and socialism anyway), and he had "sold us out to the Soviets" abroad and "sold the country down the river" at home. I cannot remember ever hearing him speak FDR's name without prefacing it with "that son of a bitch."

I became aware of Pop's political views early on. I remember lying on the floor of the sunroom listening to one of my favorite radio programs—probably "The Lone Ranger" or "The Shadow"—when an announcer broke in. It was April 12, 1945; the news flash was that President Roosevelt had died in Warm Springs, Georgia. I jumped up immediately and ran into the kitchen to tell Dear the good news. I assumed she would be ecstatic. As I recall, her reaction was much more muted than the one I had anticipated; she was never as over the top in her political views as Pop. But as I think back on it now, it is telling that I knew the basic parameters of my father's politics when I was eight years old.

I am not sure how old I was when I became aware that Pop's views on politics and race, and just about everything else for that matter, were heightened, intensified, and exaggerated by his drinking. My father had an iron will about many things. Sadly, alcohol was not one of them.

I knew about his capacity for self-discipline because of a story Dear told me when I was quite young. Pop was a heavy cigarette smoker when they were first married, and he particularly liked to smoke when he and a group of friends played cards once a week at the St. Petersburg Yacht Club. On one of these occasions, my father had nothing to drink but smoked heavily over the course of a long evening. The next morning, he woke up "feeling terrible" ("feeling like hell," Pop would have said), and he blamed what I gather resembled a bad hangover on the smoking he had done the night before. He decided to quit, cold turkey. He gave up cigarettes on the spot and never smoked again, not a single cigarette, for the rest of his life.

If he had been able to do the same with bourbon, his health and his quality of life, and indeed the quality of life for all of us, would have been dramatically improved. But Pop was an alcoholic. He was able to stop drinking periodically but never for long. I knew when those brown bags from the package store heavy with bottles of Virginia Gentleman bourbon reappeared, Pop would soon be going through a ritual we knew all too well: fix a double or triple highball as soon as he got home from the office, slide comfortably into his rocking chair in the sunroom, and down most of the contents of that tall glass in a single series of deep swallows.

The South is notoriously a land of alcohol and alcoholics. I have often wondered if it is not a land of clinical depression as well. Knowing what I know now, I am sure Pop was self-medicating and that his self-medication became an addiction. He confined his drinking to evenings at home as far as I knew, and he continued to practice law very effectively and earn a good living. But the demon that sat on his shoulder never let go. It could be banished for a while, but it always returned. When it did, I walked on eggshells around him.

Dear was aware that Pop had a drinking problem, but like most southern wives of that era, she did not challenge him with the threat to leave if he did not stop. He was never violent; he never raised a hand to her or to John or to me. And he was often in a jolly mood when he drank. But if the subject turned to politics or to race, his jaw tightened, his eyes blazed, and what I now recognize as vitriol came pouring out.

My father's political conservatism and his combustible views on race did not preclude him from having a remarkable sense of humor, however. He could crack wise with the best of them, and his wry wit was always lurking just beneath the lawyerly seriousness with which he regularly carried himself. Pop would puncture an inflated ego (particularly if it belonged to some downtown businessman) with a rapier thrust of comedic description, and he took great delight in describing himself in outlandish terms, always with a twinkle in his eye. "There is very little about which I know nothing," he would say, which was true, and he invariably added that someday he intended to teach a college course on "diverse facts" which would conclude with "a two-volume study entitled *Women I Have Known.*" This last comment came from someone who loved my mother deeply and was less likely to be a philanderer than any man who ever walked the face of the earth. When he said it, Dear would smile and roll her eyes in affectionate disbelief.

Pop also possessed a streak of kindness that was on frequent display in the course of his legal work. As his practice turned more and more toward estate law, he acquired a group of elderly widows for whom he assumed responsibility and toward whom he felt a genuine concern. He would often spend most of Saturday visiting one after another of his "Ladies," as he affectionately referred to them, to ask how they were and if there was anything they needed. When I was young I often accompanied him on these rounds, and it was clear to me that these women were devoted to my father and that his visits meant a great deal to them.

The year before I left for Woodberry, Pop thought it was time to kick my political education up a notch. In 1950, one of my father's least favorite Florida politicians, liberal United States senator Claude Pepper, a New Dealer through and through, was facing a formidable primary challenge from a Democratic congressman from Jacksonville named George Smathers. I am not sure Congressman Smathers was conservative enough to suit Pop, but it looked like he might have a chance to knock off "Red Pepper" in the primary, and that was good enough to put my father in his camp. He started taking me to nighttime political meetings, all-male and all-lawyers as far as I could tell. I remember one of his friends remarking one night, "Starting 'em off young, are you, Jack?" As I recall, my father's reply was something along the lines of "it's never too early to get 'em off on the right foot." The principle was the same one employed in raising a Confederate youth. Education began early.

I am not sure how Dear felt about all this nighttime activity. Pop was taking me regularly, at the age of thirteen, to what amounted to political smokers. But I am sure he thought the experience would do me good, to hear Smathers praised as the Second Coming and Pepper excoriated for being too cozy with communists and fellow travelers. Smathers, much to Pop's delight, won that primary, one of the bitterest in Florida's twentieth-century political history. I was too young to vote, of course, but if I had been able to, my ballot would have been cast for George Smathers "as sure as gun's made of iron" (which was Pop's phrase for a lead-pipe cinch).

So when it came to the *Brown* decision, Pop's reaction was no surprise to me. It was just one more bad choice the evil powers-that-be in Washington had made and were attempting to stuff down the throats of the American people. What was surprising, again thinking back on it now, is that he wanted my brother and me to attend Williams College in Williamstown, Massachusetts.

If there was one thing Pop believed in as deeply as his politics, it was the value of education. He had come to this conviction through his own experience. Going to the University of Virginia had changed his life, and he wanted John and me to get the same strong start that he had gotten. Pop also had a firm yardstick for what constituted an educated person: he paid particular attention to how people he met used the language, both spoken and written. On several occasions, his travels on behalf of clients had taken him to New York City. There, a disproportionate number of the men who impressed him the most, who both spoke well and wrote well, had gone to Williams. Pop had never heard of the place, but, as was his custom, he looked into it, and in this case he liked what he saw—a four-year, all-male liberal arts college nestled in a valley in the Berkshire Hills in the northwestern corner of Massachusetts. And this was particularly important to him: it had a reputation as a first-rate teaching college. Pop decided Williams would be an ideal college for his two sons.

As usual, John went first. He had pretty much assumed for most of his time at Woodberry that he would go to UVa; after three years at an all-boys school in rural Virginia, the prospect of a possible major in fraternity life in Charlottesville was an unmistakable lure. But Pop had different ideas. He told John he wanted him to go to Williams and "try it out for a year." If he did not like it, he could transfer to Virginia as a sophomore.

John never left Williams. He loved it, talked up the college, and his professors in particular, when he was home, and it seemed perfectly natural for me to follow in his footsteps (with an application in at UVa just in case). I was admitted, and in the fall of 1954, as I left St. Petersburg for Williams, I was heading north of the Mason-Dixon Line for the first time in my life.

Given the transformative impact four years at a New England college had on me, I have often wondered why Pop was such a strong advocate for Williams. Virtually no one from my hometown had ever heard of the place (the single exception was one of my father's closest friends in St. Pete, a transplant from Maine who had gone to Bowdoin). Almost everyone who went to college went either to the University of Florida or to Florida State; if you "went away" to school, it was either to Duke or Vanderbilt or, if your family happened to be Episcopalian, to Sewanee. ("Where are you going? Williams College? Where's that? Do you mean Williams & Mary?" I faced a steady barrage of such questions the summer before I left for Williamstown.)

So what prompted my father to ignore the very real possibility that he was sending his two sons into hostile territory, where the history and culture of the North, and "liberal" New England in particular, might chip away at our southern roots?

I do not have an answer to that question; I never raised it with Pop. But I have an idea. I think he considered the southern armor in which we were clad to be impenetrable. That the things he believed in so deeply, John and I believed in just as deeply. We would get a first-rate liberal arts education; we would learn to speak well and write well. But we would be impervious to change in ways that really mattered: our ideas on things like politics and race would remain grounded in the soil of the South. He knew his values were the right and proper ones. And so did we. Four years of college were not about to change what Pop referred to as "the basics"—our southern heritage and the principles and belief systems that underlay that heritage. Like the good manners with which we had been raised (Dear saw to that), he assumed that these attitudes and beliefs would survive four years away from our native South without difficulty.

Change did come for me, but it was an evolutionary process, one that seems far too slow in retrospect. The scales did not fall from my eyes the moment I stepped onto the Williams campus. Far from it. I realize now, and this realization has informed my views as a student of southern history, that what I presume was his idea—that college would not change "the basics"—was not all that far-fetched.

Two memories, both exceedingly painful, remind me of the power of those "basics."

One memory comes when I open a couple of books from my college years that still remain on my bookshelf. Both were on the syllabus of my American history course taken during the first semester of my sophomore year. One of these volumes is Benjamin Thomas's 1952 *Abraham Lincoln: A Biography*. I highlighted the passage where Thomas quotes Lincoln's comments on race in his debate with Stephen A. Douglas at Charlestown, Illinois, in 1858. "I am not, nor ever have been in favor of bringing about in any way the social and political equality of the white and black races," Lincoln said, ". . . and I will say in addition to this that there is a physical difference between the white and black races which I believe will for ever forbid the two races living together on terms of social and political equality."[7]

I am sure I noted these words in class because of something that happened shortly thereafter. The editor of a Charleston, South Carolina, newspaper came to campus to criticize the *Brown* decision and defend segregation. When I entered the hall shortly before the event started, my American history teacher, Fred Rudolph, caught sight of me and called across the room, "Charles, you should be up there on the stage with him." To say that I was embarrassed is an understatement, although I now take that embarrassment as a positive sign: at least I had begun to get an inkling that my commitment to racial segregation, to the South's Jim Crow system, might be a misplaced loyalty. My embarrassment was compounded when the defender of "the southern way of life" who was on stage delivered one of the most intellectually barren and boring talks I had ever heard, reading from the pages in a loose-leaf binder, turning them over one by one until he was blessedly finished. That, too—his miserable performance totally void of persuasive content—also got me thinking. Is *this* what I've been defending in class? I remember asking myself as I left the hall that night.

The second book from my sophomore American history syllabus was Richard Hofstadter's 1948 collection of essays entitled *The American Political Tradition and the Men Who Made It*. In his essay on John C. Calhoun, Hofstadter quotes the South Carolina senator instructing a friend back home to see to it that a runaway slave be punished with a severe whipping. Hofstadter's interpretation of this incident is what caught my eye. "The case of Aleck and the 'thirty lashes well laid on' does more for our understanding of the problem of majorities and minorities than all of Calhoun's dialectics on nullification and the concurrent majority," Hofstadter wrote.[8] My reaction to this was to pencil the following comment in the margin: "Come come, Richard, ADA got your tongue, boy!" My father had nothing but scorn for the liberal advocacy group Americans for Democratic Action. In the margin of Hofstadter's book, I had conflated Pop's political conservatism and his, and my own, and my region's, racism into one neat, seamless package.

In addition to these reminders of where I was back then, there is a second memory that, again, still forces me to cringe when I recall it. As a white southern boy, I had mastered a number of what were known in the day as "Rastus and Lulabelle" jokes. These jokes, like almost everything I heard growing up that passed for humor, were based on crude and degrading racial stereotypes. These particular jokes were told in a Negro (as we said then, if we were being polite) dialect, with a deep baritone for "Rastus" and a high falsetto for "Lulabelle." I started telling one of these jokes in a friend's room in my freshman dorm when one of our classmates passed in the hall just outside the open door. This classmate, Ted Wynne, who lived in my entry, was African American. I stopped my joke in midsentence when I realized Ted was within earshot. It was one thing to tell a dialect joke; we all did this where I came from (if you were white). It was quite another to consciously inflict direct hurt on another human being, either black or white, and to embarrass oneself at the same time. I had done both. It is small compensation now to say that I never told another "Rastus and Lulabelle" joke again, ever, either at Williams or beyond.

This incident, as painful as it is for me to describe, happened a day or two into my life at Williams. As I look back on it, I think it marked my tentative first step along a lengthy road that would carry me away from the worst of the culture of my native region. I was mortified by what had taken place on this occasion. But as my literally sophomoric reaction to the Thomas and Hofstadter readings shows clearly, my transformation—from bigot to something better than that—was slow, halting, and incomplete, a step or two forward, if I was lucky, often followed by a next step back.

My torturous emergence from racism raises one of the existential questions that lie at the heart of this book: How had I, we, all of us white southerners, become such unthinking racists to begin with? How had the tentacles of racism reached so deeply into us that we did not even know they were there, much less that these attitudes and ideas were evil and should never have been entertained in the first place?

2

The Making of a Racist

My favorite children's book when I was growing up was entitled *Ezekiel,* written by a white Floridian named Elvira Garner. This slender volume was published in New York by Henry Holt and Company in 1937, the year I was born (Canadian distribution was by Oxford University Press).

The first story in the book opens this way:

"Away down in Sanford, Florida dar lives a lil' cullerd boy, an' he names Ezekiel. An' dis boy he live wid he Pappy an' he Mammy an' he Sister Emancipation, an' he brudder Lil' Plural an' Assafetida, de baby."

I took endless delight in Ezekiel's adventures on "de St. John's Ribber," as he caught a "big ole cat-fish" in this opening story, unsuccessfully looked for work on a steamboat ("Lil' nigger boy, you too small," the "Cap'n" told him), but, through persistence and politeness, landed a job for "he Pappy" on the self-same vessel, "a-rollin' an' a-totin' an' a-draggin' things onto ole freight boat."

This opening chapter, like all of the six stories in the book, is illustrated by the author's watercolor drawings of stick figures with coal black faces acting out passages in the text, such as Ezekiel "got lil' ole fishin' pole outen de shed," while "Emancipation went 'long pullin' de baby in lil' ole cyart" and "Lil' Plural toten' de bait can."

Each chapter—each individual story—also ends with a four-line song, also in dialect, such as this one at the end of chapter 1:

Ole ribber run norf, an don' run souf.
Ole cat-fish he tas'e fine!
Pappy got a dandy job
On de St. John's Ribber Line.

My earliest childhood memory, literally the first thing I can recall about my life, is sitting in my mother's lap having her read these stories to me.

After this opening chapter, our plucky, intrepid hero's boyhood adventures continue:

Ezekiel talking his way onto a field-work gang "settin' celery" ("Miss Little Sister," his crew boss, "is pow'ful large"—Garner's drawing shows a very heavy-set African American woman standing arms akimbo).

Ezekiel searching for a "Chris'mus tree big nuff to hol' all dat you say Santy gwine bring."

Ezekiel going "to de big fair to Orlando," where a sideshow barker, "a fine white gem'man," displays the baby, Assafetida, up on stage as a "genuine golliwog from the wilds of Ethiopia."

Ezekiel looking for buried treasure ("Spanish gem'man bury de' big box er' gol' in swamp . . . an' ain' never cum back to git hit").

Ezekiel listening to tales told by "Unc Adam Joshua," who "say he nigh 'bout hundered year ole"—stories of "Injuns" and "a gret big 'gaitor" and "Brer Mockin' Bird" (but, strangely enough, not a word about slavery).

I am certain that Dear and I used to sing the songs sprinkled throughout the book because the lyrics to one of these contains two penciled additions in my mother's beautiful handwriting:

      ole
To hear ^ Jordan roll.
Roll Jordan, roll,
Roll Jordan, roll.

Ah wants to go to Heabin when Ah die,

ole
To hear ^ Jordan roll.

And I am sure we sang these songs in dialect; Dear inserted "ole," not "old," to conform to lines like "Ah wants to go to Heabin when Ah die."[1]

In 1991, John and I were going through our house in St. Petersburg after Dear's death when I spotted *Ezekiel* in a small hall bookcase just outside the "baby room." I recognized it the moment I saw it, and I was flooded with a mixture of emotions as soon as I opened it—those wonderful childhood memories of Dear reading to me, immense sadness at her recent death, and absolute, appalling amazement at the content of these stories, the dialect in which they were told, and the drawings that accompanied the text.

I now realize that this book was the beginning of a long process of my education as a southerner, particularly my acculturation into the white South's racial attitudes. There was nothing mean or malevolent in Dear's reading these stories to me; I do not believe she had a mean or malevolent bone in her body. She was also highly intelligent. As Pop would say, she "wasn't hiding behind the barn when the brains were handed out" (later, when I was at Woodberry and kidded her about going to "finishing school," she laughed and said if she had, she would not have had to read so much Proust). In addition to being smart, she was also gentle, thoughtful, empathetic, and compassionate. I am not overselling her here in the slightest; everyone who knew her would agree with this description. But she was also someone brought up in a place and time when whites did not consider these portrayals of African Americans either offensive or outlandish. Indeed, just the opposite was true. I am sure she found these stories totally appropriate for a white mother to read to her son as soon as he was able to enjoy them. And enjoy them I did.

And this is what I *learned* from them:

Colored folks are funny.

Colored folks talk funny.

Their names are funny.

Their antics are funny.

Their physical appearance and movements and gaudy, ill-fitting clothes are funny. Those stick figures conveyed all of this, even though their faces were anonymous and almost totally devoid of definition. Only occasionally could one make out what appeared to be a grin on a figure shown in profile, and their hair was spiked and sticking out from the back of their heads.

Most of all, colored folks are different from us white folks—different in color, different in speech, different in ways too numerous to mention, a "different breed of cat," as my father would put it. And because colored folks are so profoundly different, the next step came easy: colored folks are inferior.

These early messages received confirmation everywhere I looked.

I realize now that many of the Jim Crow customs I learned growing up I absorbed more through a process of osmosis than through verbal instruction. I was, to quote a religious phrase (not inappropriate given the transcendent importance of maintaining proper racial etiquette at all times), simply bearing witness to what was going on every day all around me.

There were two jelly glasses and two sets of chipped, orange-colored china—plates, bowls, cups and saucers—in a separate corner of one of our kitchen cupboards. They were used exclusively by Ed, the black man who mowed our lawn, and by Illinois, the black woman who cleaned our house, did our laundry, ironed our sheets, and sometimes cooked our dinner.

I learned very quickly that I should use the nice tiled bathroom on the second floor of our house. The not-so-nicely appointed half bath off the back porch—wooden floor, small sink attached to the wall, white paint on the toilet seat so worn the wood showed through—was for Illinois and Ed. Our two bathrooms did not have signs, ubiquitous on public restrooms across the southern landscape, reading "White" and "Colored" over the doors, but it would have been perfectly appropriate if they had.

I learned never to shake hands with an African American person. Pop never did, Dear never did, so I never did.

I addressed African American men and women who worked for us by their first names. I did not use their last names prefaced by Mr. or Mrs. or Miss because my parents never did.

I learned, on a morning I shall never forget, that African Americans arriving at our house should always use the back doors.

Lillian Smith wrote in her magnificent autobiography *Killers of the Dream* that white children growing up in the Jim Crow South always experienced a moment of revelation, a flash of lightning that illuminated in a blinding instant what segregation means.[2] (Of course, as Anne Moody tells us in her equally brilliant autobiography *Coming of Age in Mississippi,* black children experienced the same lightning flash but from the perspective of the oppressed, not the oppressor.)[3] The day a black man came to the wrong door of our house was my day of Jim Crow lightning.

I was eight years old. It was 1945, and World War II had recently ended. We had just started using the car again following the end of wartime rationing, and I remember very well the first two times we took anything approaching a frivolous drive: the first was V-E Day and the second was V-J Day. On these two occasions, the four of us piled into our 1939 Buick and headed downtown to celebrate our victories over Nazi Germany and the Empire of Japan. We circled St. Pete's premier tourist attraction, our mammoth (as it seemed to me) "Million Dollar Pier," honking our horn, waving from the windows, and yelling our heads off. And in the following weeks, Pop was driving to his office again and dropping me off at North Ward School on his way to work.

On the morning in question, the black man who owned Bill's Shoe Shine Parlor had come to our house to make an apology to my father. Bill's business was located in an arcade off an alley near the Florida National Bank Building, where Pop had his office. I am not sure what prompted the need for an apology, but I strongly suspect one of Bill's shoeshine "boys" (most were grown men) had said something that offended my father or Pop had simply heard an offhand comment one of them had made and had taken objection to it. Whatever the reason, Pop had clearly stormed off in anger. My father went to Bill's often to get his handsome, two-toned spectators shined, and Bill (I never learned his last name) obviously did not want to lose Pop's patronage.

We kept our car under a porte cochere on the west side of our house and accessed the car every morning through a side door just off our living room. Bill was waiting just outside that door. I heard him say, "Mr. Dew, I'm really sorry . . ." He never got to finish that sentence. Pop tore into him with an explosive verbal assault that was unlike anything I had ever heard before. Bill had committed the unpardonable sin of coming to the wrong door. I had never seen my father so angry, had never seen him react to anything or anyone with such fury. I do not remember his words. I think I was too frightened to register what he was yelling at Bill. But I remember his face and his voice and his rage. Bill withdrew immediately, and as far as I know, Pop never had his shoes shined at Bill's again.

The lesson I received from this searing incident was clear: a black person coming to our house had one place and one place only he or she was permitted to knock: the back door.

I realize now that my father's racial views and his political opinions were joined at the hip. I was not as aware of that back then as I am now, but I got a glimpse of the connection in 1950 when I was thirteen and Pop brought home a small paperback book that took dead aim at Eleanor Roosevelt.

This particular publication was entitled *Weep No More, My*

Our home at 234 25th Avenue North, St. Petersburg, Florida. The side door from our living room and the porte cochere, where we kept our car, are to the right.

Lady, and it carried on the front cover a caricature of a buck-toothed Mrs. Roosevelt crying crocodile tears. The cover also provided this verbal description: "A Southerner Answers Mrs. Roosevelt's Report on the 'Poor and Unhappy' South." The author, and publisher, was identified as W. E. Debnam of Raleigh, North Carolina, and the Graphic Press, Inc., also of Raleigh, printed the book. The price was fifty cents, but orders by mail required a dollar for two copies, plus ten cents postage and mailing charge, sent to the author's home address, which was conveniently provided on the copyright page. By 1953, three years after this little volume first appeared, it had reached its twelfth printing, and author Debnam claimed there were 210,000 copies in print.

My father loved this little book. He kept a copy in his bookcase in the sunroom and referred to it often. Debnam's effort was prompted by Mrs. Roosevelt's comments about the South in her column, "My Day," which was widely syndicated in newspapers around the country. This particular column followed a trip to Chapel Hill, where Mrs. Roosevelt had spoken at a forum sponsored by the University of North Carolina.

After complimenting the "charm about the South" and the "smell of magnolias" and "the less harried" pace of life, as well as "the grace of living," the former First Lady had the audacity to say that "underneath it all, I'm not so sure that there are not signs of poverty and unhappiness that will gradually have to disappear if that part of the nation is going to prosper and keep pace with the rest of it."

This latter statement was enough to set the author off. The rest of the book is a diatribe directed at northern do-gooders who look down their elongated blue noses at poor, benighted Dixie. Adding insult to injury, these spiteful outsiders fail to see the corruption and stench of their own Yankee neighborhoods, like "that great Negro ghetto in the heart of New York that is Harlem," which Debnam graciously described as "possibly the greatest cesspool of heaped-up-and-pressed-down-and-running-over poverty and crime and spiritual and moral and economic unhappiness on the face of the earth."

I think the reader can catch the author's drift. Any shortcomings that the South might manifest, beginning with Black Reconstruction and continuing on to the present day, Debnam laid at the feet of northern exploitation. Reconstruction, "the South's Gethsemane," was particularly heinous, and the public looting and government corruption were not the worst of it. That dubious honor belonged to the hitherto unknown *fifth* "Horseman of the Apocalypse . . . the Horseman whose name is Fear—astride a horse of Federal blue." In a thinly veiled reference to the threat posed by black men breaching the sexual color line, Debnam described the desperate plight of southern white men in these terms: "It's the Fear of defenseless men facing a foe who strikes by stealth, not against one's own person, but against the person of his loved ones and the sanctity of his home." And, of course, the Yankee invaders had encouraged these black animals when they "ate with them and slept with them and danced with them and invited them into their homes."[4]

This brief picture of Reconstruction in *Weep No More, My Lady,* and particularly the last line quoted just above, gives me an opportunity to raise one of the critical issues, perhaps *the* critical issue, on the minds of white southerners of my day and time. Debnam's language and description—"Fear" with a capital "F," references to northerners eating and dancing and sleeping with "liberated slaves"—these words were much more than a history lesson. It was a warning to the contemporary South, to my South, to those of us who were responsible for manning the barricades of segregation in the present time. Do not, under any circumstances, let black men through your front door. If you do, they will end up in your bedroom.

I am not sure when I became aware of the sexual threat supposedly posed by black men. I know I learned this at some point, we all did, white boys and white girls. I sometimes think this visceral dread was bred into the marrow of our bones. It was, at its most primal level, the fear of a black seed in a white womb. I know I was not taught this fear the way I was taught other things about race. I did not read books like *Ezekiel* or *Eneas Africanus* (which will be discussed shortly) about it. But it was implicit in my *Youth's Confederate Primer* when the threat of slave insurrection was raised. And W. E. Debnam made it explicit in his screed against Eleanor Roosevelt, although he set the circumstances for black-white sexual contact in the post–Civil War South and blamed dissolute Yankees for this assault on civilized values. Neither my father nor my mother ever sat me down and explained to me why black men posed such a danger. But I did learn of this existential threat, and

I am sure I learned it at a fairly young age. I knew what Debnam was talking about when I read those words about Reconstruction.

So if there is one point about the South in which I grew up that readers need to understand, it is this: nothing, absolutely nothing, was more important to white southerners, and particularly white southern men, than defending the purity of white southern womanhood.

This concern for female virtue ran in only one direction, of course. Whites considered all black women promiscuous "Jezebels" who lured white men to their beds and who got what they deserved (why else would the age of consent for girls in South Carolina be ten years old until 1895, when it was raised to fourteen?[5] How else can we explain the stunningly brilliant W. J. Cash making reference in *The Mind of the South* to "the sidelong glance of the all-complaisant Negro woman"?[6]). No, logical consistency was not an attribute with which white southern males were overly concerned. The *white* side of the sexual color line was the ultimate line of defense. Lynch mobs were turned loose because of it. Race riots were launched because of it. The entire Jim Crow superstructure existed because of it. The sexual color line was the be-all and end-all for us. And it had been that way for a very long time.

The intersection of race and sex in white southern culture is something I have written about extensively in my scholarship, and I do not think it is necessary to go into elaborate detail about it here.[7] It might, however, be appropriate to offer very modest documentation to illustrate my point about the deep historical roots of this fear.

Thomas Jefferson wrote in 1785 that in ancient Rome "emancipation required but one effort. The slave, when made free, might mix with, without staining the blood of his master." Not so in the South: "[W]ith us a second is necessary, unknown to history. When freed, he is to be removed beyond reach of mixture."[8]

Senator Albert Gallatin Brown of Mississippi warned his constituents in October 1860 that Republican-led abolition meant that "the negro . . . shall go to the white man's table, and the white man to his—that he shall share the white man's bed, and the white man his—that his son shall marry the white man's daughter, and the white man's daughter his son."[9]

In 1945, Senator Theodore G. Bilbo of Mississippi condemned Franklin D. Roosevelt's Fair Employment Practices Committee as "nothing but a plot to put niggers to work next to your daughters."[10]

Four years later, another Mississippian, Congressman John Bell Williams, insisted that scheming American communists and their misguided liberal allies were masking "the rotten stench of their insidious aims under an outward cloak of purity miscalled 'Civil Rights'" and were actually "attempting to bring about a forced amalgamation of the white and black races."[11]

In his inaugural address as governor of Alabama in 1963, George Corley Wallace charged that white southerners were being betrayed by northern liberals who were committed to the "false doctrine of communistic amalgamation." If left unchecked, this pernicious doctrine would result in the creation of a "mongrel unit of one" in the South, "under a single all powerful government."[12]

These quotes could be repeated almost ad nauseam. My point is this: as a young white man being raised in the Jim Crow South, I was being brought into a hallowed white male brotherhood whether I was conscious of it or not. I was learning to fear and abhor the sexual contamination of white southern females by black male predators. Never mind that this threat was utter nonsense. The fear was there, or, as W. E. Debnam put it, the "Fear." And *any* chink in the solid wall of segregation—swimming pools, buses, libraries, you name it, and, God help us, the schools (where black boys and white girls would rub elbows with each other)—would lead in the end to the same dire consequence: the sexual violation of the color line. This expectation was a major reason why white

southerners viewed even the slightest concession toward integration as the beginning of the great unraveling, the pulled thread
that would eventually bring the whole Jim Crow tapestry crashing
down. As the historian Edward Ayers has perceptively noted, once
segregation began in earnest in the late nineteenth century, there
was no logical place to stop.[13] The same was true of integration,
white southerners believed. Not even the slightest inch could be
given; if it were, the full mile would inevitably follow. At the end of
that unthinkable road was the proverbial "fate worse than death"
for white southern females. In the nineteenth century, "amalgamation" was the word one dare not speak. In the twentieth century,
it was "miscegenation."

In the closing pages of *Weep No More, My Lady*, author Debnam adds a final salient to the South's defensive perimeter on
race. Northerners should keep their cotton-pickin' hands off the
South. "We're making progress—real progress—toward better
racial understanding in the South, but it's going to take time—a
lot of time," he insisted. And "this constant barrage of criticism
by persons outside the South" like you, Mrs. Roosevelt, he concluded, was "one of the greatest road-blocks in the way of better
understanding and cooperation between the races—as every man
of good will in the South both Negro and white will tell you."[14] So,
listen up, you Yankees: no more Reconstructions, no more outside
interference. And stuff a sock in the criticism.

I am not sure when I read *Weep No More, My Lady*, but I did
at some point, and I thought it made an excellent argument for
southerners (read white southerners) being allowed to solve the
race problem in their own good time (which meant more or less
never). And Dear certainly agreed with Pop and me about this and
about Yankee hypocrisy and pretty much everything else Debnam
said. Northerners had been beating up on the South for far too
long, and they had their own dirty linen to wash out before they
came down to tell us how to deal with any of ours.

In retrospect, nothing displays the pervasive influence of the Jim Crow ethos more clearly to me than the effect it had on my mother. As I noted earlier, she was a kind, compassionate, deeply religious person. And yet Dear could be as unyielding on matters of race as my father. She would never display the anger he manifested on that all-too-memorable morning when Bill came to our house, and she would never use the language he used. John and I were forbidden to say the word "nigger," even though Pop used it often, as did my Grandmother Dew (which probably accounts for some of the ease with which my father uttered the word). Dear tried to teach us to say "nigra," which I came to realize later was a pronunciation favored in genteel white circles in the Jim Crow South. But John and I stuck with "Negro," probably because this is what Illinois said, and we both spent a great deal of time around her when we were growing up.

Dear was convinced that segregation was "best for both races," as she put it. She genuinely believed that black folks were happy on their side of the color line. Any trouble could be traced to the NAACP (it took me a while before I learned that those initials stood for the National Association for the Advancement of Colored People). Invariably, she embraced paternalism as the right and proper way to deal with the black men, women, and children with whom she came into personal contact.

The housing situation faced by Illinois and her husband brought this paternalistic quality to the fore when I was in my teens. Illinois was married to a man named Joe Culver, who worked as a "porter" (I was never sure what that meant) at a barbershop downtown. They lived in a rundown rental property, one of many owned by one of my father's clients—torn screens on the windows, indifferent plumbing that sometimes worked and more often did not, sagging steps, leaky roof, just about anything and everything that came with segregated housing in Methodist Town, the black section of St. Petersburg where Illinois and Joe lived.

When the city government considered implementing some housing codes that would force landlords ("slumlords" would be the more appropriate word here) to upgrade their rental properties, my father went before the city council to argue on behalf of his client against such an ordinance. Yet Illinois and Joe were clearly being victimized by their housing situation. I remember Illinois telling Dear one morning that the torn screens on her house were letting in so many mosquitoes that she and Joe could not sleep at night. Dear and Pop decided they would do something about their housing situation and came up with a plan. They would arrange for Illinois and Joe to buy their own home. I was never sure of the financial aspects surrounding this transaction—some combination of gift and loan, I suspect—but the Culvers were able to get out of the rattrap in which they were living and into a decent home.

I know it was a decent home because I was the only member of my family ever to cross the threshold. After I got my driver's license, I used to drive Illinois home on a regular basis. One day, she asked me if I would like to come in and see where she and Joe lived. I said sure and accompanied her up the front steps and through her front door. I walked into a modestly furnished but impeccably clean living room and stopped as Illinois paused to give me a chance to take it all in. Her pride was palpable. As I recall, I complimented her on the way the living room looked and said something about how nice the house was, gave her dog, a large, black, friendly mixed breed named Smudge, a pat, and then I left and drove back to my house.

When I mentioned to my mother that I had gone to look at Illinois's home and seen her living room, she made me sit down and describe to her exactly what I had seen in as much detail as I could possibly remember.

Only later did I get a sense of what had gone on here. Illinois knew there was no way she could invite Dear into her house, but she wanted my mother and father to know that she and Joe had made a good home. I was the messenger. It was all right for me, a teenage white kid, to walk in, but my parents were another matter altogether. The same racial etiquette that brought Illinois to the back door of our house did not permit my mother to walk even through the front door of hers.

In 1951, the same year I turned fourteen and received my .22, my *Lee's Lieutenants,* and my *Youth's Confederate Primer,* my mother gave me a small, paper-covered book entitled *Eneas Africanus.* The author was a man named Harry Stillwell Edwards, and the book was originally published in 1920 by the J. W. Burke Company of Macon, Georgia; my edition carried a reprint date of 1951.

As I recall, it was not any sort of special gift, certainly not a birthday present. I remember receiving those all at once, and Dear's gift came later that year. She just loved the book, I think, and felt that I would, too.

Essentially, *Eneas Africanus* is a more adult version of the *Ezekiel* tales—amusing, affectionate, in its way, toward the caricatured black central character, and heavily reliant for its humor on the foibles and eccentric speech patterns of the fictional Eneas Africanus. And, again, very much like *Ezekiel,* it is deeply racist.

The book is sitting on my desk as I write this. My junior high, Palmer Method signature is on the inside front cover. The frontispiece is a sepia-tinted sketch, in profile, of an aged, white-haired black man, with a white beard covering the bottom half of his face. His eyes are almost closed and his lips are pressed tightly together, as if he were facing into a stiff wind. The caption under this picture reads "Eneas Africanus, the fast vanishing type."

The "fast vanishing type" this fictional character represented was what was known as "Sambo," or the "faithful darkie," when I was growing up. Southern stereotypes about male African Americans had undergone a seesaw effect in the late nineteenth and into the twentieth century. The antebellum "Sambo" had given way to the menacing "black beast rapist" of Thomas Dixon's best-selling 1905 novel *The Clansman* (the book on which D. W. Griffith based his enormously successful 1915 film *Birth of a Nation*). But by the 1920s, the dominant image had reverted back to what the historian Joel Williamson calls the "neo-Sambo" stereotype, or, closer to what I heard in my earlier years, the "faithful darkie."[15] This stock figure was inherently lazy, mischievous, often a teller of tall tales, and not very bright, but he knew his proper place in society and was devoted to his white folks, dependent on them for guidance and the patronage that put bread on his table (and, on occasion, offered protection from lynch mobs composed of poor white crackers). "Sambo" spoke in a thick, almost impenetrable, dialect, garbled his syntax, and was capable of producing hilarious malapropisms. When John S. Tilley, author of my *Youth's Confederate Primer,* described slaves as "childlike, good natured, well-behaved" hands, he was articulating, in near-perfect capsule form, the essential qualities of this stereotype.

This caricature of the dim-witted black man-child (i.e., "boy") had been around for a very long while in the minds of white southerners. Before the years between about 1890 and 1915, the era Joel Williamson calls the period of "Radical racism"—the years of Dixon's venomous novels, out-of-control lynching, and the bloody Atlanta race riot of 1906—"Sambo" had been the dominant black male stereotype.[16] Some three decades before the Civil War, my ancestor, Thomas Roderick Dew, astute fellow that he was, described this white southern image with remarkable clarity. The enslaved people of his beloved Southland "form the happiest portion of our society," he wrote in 1832. "A merrier being does not exist on the face of the globe than the negro slave of the United States." This southern Eden faced an omnipresent danger, however, a malevolent force to be kept at bay at all cost—the Yankee abolitionist. "Sambo" was loyal and lovable most of the time, Dew continued, but those vile northerners could transform "the most harmless and happy creature that lives on earth . . . into a dark designing and desperate rebel."[17]

If one were to strike the word "slave" after "negro" in the first of Dew's passages quoted above and substitute "integrationist" for "rebel" in the second, and cloak the twentieth-century villain in the garb of the NAACP (instead of Garrisonian broadcloth), Dew's words could, and probably would, have been used to describe the state of race relations in the South by every adult white person I knew when I was growing up. Our black folks, our "Sambos," our "faithful darkies," were "harmless and happy," again to use T. R. Dew's words, but God save us if those villainous outside agitators ever got ahold of them.

So what was the story of Eneas Africanus, this "fast vanishing type"?

The "Author's Preface" sets the stage beautifully. "Dear to the hearts of the [white] Southerners, young and old, is the vanishing type, conspicuous in Eneas of this record; and as in a sidelight herein are seen the [white] Southerners themselves, kind of heart, tolerant and appreciative of the humor and pathos of the Negro's life," Harry Stillwell Edwards wrote. "Eneas would have been arrested in any country other than the South," he continued, but the aged Negro "could have traveled his life out as the guest of his 'white folks'" in the American South. "Is this story true?" Edwards asked at the end of this brief introduction. "Everybody says it is."[18]

The story begins with an 1872 advertisement supposedly placed in newspapers across the South by one George E. Tommey, "Late Major, Tommey's Legion, C. S. A." (we are soon told that "next to General Joseph Johnston," Major Tommey was "the bravest man in the Georgia armies"). The good Major is seeking the return of a silver "Bride's Cup," entrusted to "an old family Negro" for transportation to a safe place in 1864 as Sherman's troops approached Tommeyville, the family homestead. The "old family Negro" is, of course, Eneas Africanus, described as "a small grey-haired old fellow and very talkative."[19]

Major Tommey's only daughter, eighteen-year-old Beauregarde Forrest ("a petite brunette of great beauty" whose name has been changed by an "act of the Georgia Legislature . . . in honor of the two heroes of the Confederacy, dear to the heart of her illustrious father"), is about to be married, and for generations every bride in the family has taken a drink of pure water from that cup on her wedding day. The promise of such a draft is engraved on the cup: "A happy grandchile on each knee" will surely follow.

Eneas Africanus and the cup have disappeared, and now, eight years after he was last seen leaving the plantation in a loaded wagon pulled by an old mare named Lady Chain, Major Tommey is desperately looking for the missing Bride's Cup.

The story unfolds in a series of letters sparked by the Major's advertisement, and it soon becomes evident that Eneas has become hopelessly confused and is looking literally all over the South for "Thomasville" instead of "Tommeyville" (the "confused freedman" was a variant on the "faithful darkie" stereotype in the years following the end of the Civil War). Eneas's travels have taken him (a map is helpfully provided to trace his wanderings) to Florida, Alabama, Mississippi, Tennessee, and finally to North and South Carolina as the fateful wedding day approaches.

Do Eneas and the cup arrive in time? Of course they do! (How often do historians get to use an exclamation point?) A newspaper reporter, present to cover the wedding, gives us the scene.

"In the red light of the bonfire an old Negro suddenly appeared," and the black and white crowd, assembled to watch the wedding, rushes forward. It is, naturally, Eneas Africanus.

"'Eneas, you black rascal, where have you been?'" the Major shouts.

"'Oh, Lord! Marse George! Glory be ter God! Out o' de wilderness! De' projekin son am back ergin!'" cries Eneas.

"'Where have you been, sir?'" the Major asks, "... choking with tears and laughter."

"'All over the blessed worl', Marse George! But I'm home ergin!—You hyar me, Niggers?—home ergin!—'"

Eneas has not only returned with the Bride's Cup, he has also remarried and has brought with him his new wife and "a small colony of children," who tumble out of the wagon "like cooters from a log."

"'I done brought you a whole bunch o' new Yallerhama, Burningham Niggers, Marse George! Some folks tell me dey is free, but I know dey b'long ter Marse Tommey, des like Lady Chain and her colt!'" Eneas adds proudly.

To bring this touching story to a close, the bride and groom ("Mirabeau Lamar Temple, of Dallas, Tex.") drink from the cup, displaying much joy and appropriate embarrassment at the expectation that progeny will soon be forthcoming.

In the final scene, Eneas (who departed in 1864 with "all the Confederate money the family [had] left") tries to return his remaining funds to "Marse George."

"'Keep it, Eneas,' said the Major, almost exploding with laughter, and patting the old man on the shoulder, 'that bunch of Burningham Yallerhama Niggers more than squares us.'"[20]

I do not think very much explication is required at this point about *Eneas Africanus*. To repeat a point made earlier, much the same comments could be offered about this story as were offered when *Ezekiel* was discussed at the beginning of this chapter, although the supposed humor involved in Eneas's insistence that his children—that "whole bunch o' new Yallerhama, Burningham Niggers"—are slaves belonging to "Marse George," just "like Lady Chain and her colt," goes well beyond the most offensive of the countless racist elements in the *Ezekiel* stories. I think the main thing that needs to be said is that my education into the ways of the white South continued as I grew older. What was presented to me as a child in the *Ezekiel* tales was presented to me again as a teenage boy in *Eneas Africanus*. It was a process of repetition and reinforcement, not in any necessarily didactic sense, but just something that occurred in the normal course of my growing up on the white side of the color line in the Jim Crow South. "Charles loved the *Ezekiel* stories," I can hear Dear saying to herself, "and I'll bet he'll enjoy *Eneas Africanus,* too." And, of course, I did back then, very much.

As should be evident by now, there was an extraordinary circulation of these distinctly regional publications back when I was younger. As was the case with the *Youth's Confederate Primer* and *Weep No More, My Lady,* books like *Eneas Africanus* were publicized by word of mouth and passed from hand to hand among white southerners, and I suspect they had a considerable influence in forming that elusive thing known as public opinion. I know they influenced opinion in my household. And I happen to think these little volumes deserve much more serious scholarly scrutiny than they have received. In that pre-Internet era, they served as the equivalent of a Jim Crow blogosphere, confirming crude and outrageous stereotypes, validating sulfurous misinformation and historical myth, and elevating our prejudices and our bigotries to the status of revealed truth.

One point in the story of Eneas's journey triggered a memory in me, something I literally had not thought about for many years.

When Eneas first returns, he refers to himself as "De' projekin son." This mangling of "prodigal" made me remember a phonograph record Pop brought home one day when I was probably eight or nine years old. The record was entitled "The Peasel Tree Sermon," but it had very little identifying information beyond that—no record company label, for example. It was supposed to be a recording of a sermon a Negro preacher came up with spontaneously after "letin' de' Bible drap op'n" and taking as his text the first thing that caught his eye (I am asking the reader's indulgence here; I am writing in dialect to try to convey how these words sounded to me):

"An' de' chil'en of Isre'l wharsh'p de' Lawd wit de' harp, and wit de' inst'ument of de' seben strings, an' wit de,' an' wit de' p-s-a-l-t-r-e. Hmmm. 'P-s-a-l-t-r-e.' An' wit de,' an' wit de' *Peasel Tree*!"

The entire sermon then becomes a series of elaborate, totally made-up "biblical" tales based on the preacher's misreading of the word "psaltre." The magical "Peasel Tree" plays a key role in all sorts of wondrous doings, and as a boy, I was fascinated and endlessly amused by these fabulous tales.

I even memorized long passages. I had a reasonably good ear for mimicry, and I mastered the preacher's dialect well enough to entertain the entire Dew family—aunts, uncles, cousins, Grandmother Dew, all of us—when we would gather in one of our homes for Thanksgiving and Christmas, which we did every year when I was growing up.

Our recording of "The Peasel Tree Sermon" has long since disappeared, but I can still remember snatches of some of those passages, and one story line I can recall in some detail.

The Children of Israel are being held in bondage in Egypt, and Moses employs the Peasel Tree to try to secure their release (again, I request the reader's indulgence as I attempt to re-create what I heard and memorized):

"Moses, he cut a limb from de' Peasel Tree, an' he say, 'I'm gwine make a staf' from dat limb an' walk up to Mr. Pharaoh's front do' an' tell him to turn my people loose.'"

"Now, Mr. Pharaoh, he be's quality white folks, in dem times, and dem parts, an' Moses, he walk up to Mr. Pharaoh's front do', an' he bang on dat do' wit de' Peasel Tree staf'."

"An' Mr. Pharaoh, he cum to de' do' an' he say, 'Moses, what you doin' cummin' up to white folk's front do'?'"

"An' Moses, he say, 'Mr. Pharaoh, I wants you to turn my people loose.'"

"An' Mr. Pharaoh, he say, 'I ain't gwine do it, Moses.'"

"An' Moses, he say, '*Mr. Pharaoh*! I wants you to turn my people *loose*!'"

"An' Mr. Pharaoh, he say, 'Moses, how many times I got to tel' you, I ain't gwine do it!'"

"An' den Moses, he cast dat' Peasel Tree staf' down to de' groun', and it turn into a *fiery serpent*!"

"An' Mr. Pharaoh, he say, 'Moses, now dat I's thinkin' on it, dem chillin' of Isre'l is mighty po' field hands, ain't worth much no how. I's gwine turn 'em loose!'"

Having accomplished this first step, Moses then employs the Peasel Tree to part the Red Sea so that the Israelites can cross. He mounts the Peasel Tree in a sturdy wagon to lead the way:

"'I wants dat wagon pul'ed by a couple o' big Missouri mules,' Moses say. 'Don't hitch up any o' dem shamblin' liddle cotton field mules to dat wagon!'"

And, pulled by those big Missouri mules, the Peasel Tree clears a path through the Red Sea and leads the Children of Israel to the Promised Land.

When I delivered my holiday recitations, I was probably nine or ten years old. (I suspect one reason I remember this story is because of the reference to Moses coming to the front door of Pharaoh's house; the incident involving my father and Bill was never too far from my conscious state.)

I am not proud to tell this story, but I do so to make a point: like *Ezekiel* and *Eneas Africanus,* there was nothing about "The Peasel Tree Sermon" that any of us found in the slightest degree offensive. In fact, just the opposite was true: we all found it very funny and thoroughly entertaining. Based as it was on black stereotypes almost universally accepted by white southerners back then, it was like telling a "Rastus and Lulabelle" joke shorn of the risqué elements. We all did it. We all laughed at it. And we all thought nothing of it.

White amusement over black language was omnipresent in the South in which I grew up. In our house, all of us were aware of certain words and speech mannerisms Illinois used regularly, and we adopted many of them, smilingly, into our family vocabulary.

She would invert the two parts of some words—"boxcars" would become "carboxes" and "grasshoppers" would become "hoppergrasses," for example. If someone was overweight, they were "rich looking." My brother, John, who was rapidly growing into his six-foot-plus frame, was "big limbded." If she happened to be in the kitchen in the late afternoon when our big basset hound, Rascal, started begging for his dinner, she would observe that "he be's hongry." Illinois told us she and Joe had begun to leave their dog, Smudge, in the house when they went to work because some boys in the neighborhood had started "chunkin' at him" if they left him outside. If one of us looked particularly good one day, Illinois would compliment us by saying we "just looked so fine," with an emphasis on the "fine." We used these words and phrases all the time, never in the presence of Illinois, but they became a part of my family's way of speaking.

Over the years, I have wondered about how I should think about this. Our amusement—the smiles that would come to our faces when we spoke as she did—was in some ways a mark of our affection for her, but I have come to believe that this was the sort of affection one would extend to a family pet. By mimicking her, we were patronizing her, not in any mean sense, but we were patronizing her nonetheless. And human beings normally do not patronize those we consider our equals.

I have written in some detail about Illinois to this point but have had very little to say about Ed, the African American man who worked at our home. The primary reason for this neglect is that I remember very little about him. He came to our house once a week to cut the grass (with a hand-pushed mower), put in a full day's work, and then we did not see him again until the following week. I did not even know his last name. Illinois, by contrast, was at our house several times a week, and John and I interacted with her constantly. The one clear memory I have about Ed is not directly associated with his presence; it was triggered by his absence.

I am not sure how old I was when this happened, probably eight or nine, but Ed failed to show up for work one day, and Illinois told us he had had to be hospitalized. I cannot recall if I ever learned the cause, but Ed obviously was facing some sort of health trouble. The hospital, Mercy Hospital, was, of course, a Jim Crow facility.

My father called Mercy Hospital to see how Ed was doing, and I happened to overhear Pop's side of the conversation.

I was almost as surprised by what he said and how he said it as I had been to hear him explode at Bill years earlier. Pop stammered, he could not find the right words to say what he wanted to say, he sounded confused and inarticulate. I had never heard him speak that way before. He was normally supremely self-confident when he spoke, chose his words carefully and well, "a man of round conterdunction," as he liked to describe himself (using a word he may well have invented—I never heard anyone else use it, before or since). He was anything but a "man of round conterdunction" on this occasion.

I assume this conversation ended when my father found out what he wanted to know, but I am not certain. What I remember distinctly was his profound unease.

I think I know what was going on here. Pop was dealing with a black professional on the other end of the phone, with an educated, trained hospital employee. And he had absolutely no idea how to talk to this person. He was used to dealing with servants coming to our home (or, in the case of Bill, someone who tried to come to our home the wrong way). The person at Mercy Hospital was, again to use one of Pop's favorite phrases, a very "different breed of cat." And he was supremely uncomfortable in this situation.

I do not remember seeing very much of Ed after this; his health problem may have been a serious one. What I do remember was my father's severe discomfort when he tried to find out what that problem was.

If there was one thing in my youthful education as a racist that offered a push in the direction of inclusion and genuine appreciation of black culture, it was the radio. I loved to listen to the radio. I even persuaded Dear and Pop to let me have a small radio on my bedside table. At night, when I was ten or eleven years old and was supposed to be trying to go to sleep, I would scan the dial looking for something to listen to. One night, I discovered WLAC.[21]

These call letters were carried by a clear-channel 50,000-watt radio station in Nashville that broadcast an amazingly strong signal into my part of the South. In the evenings, the disc jockeys—I remember Gene Nobles, "Hoss" Allen, and "John R"—played what I soon learned were "rhythm and blues" records. The music and the musicians were amazing. B. B. ("Blues Boy," the DJs called him) King, Muddy Waters, Howlin' Wolf, Little Walter, John Lee Hooker—I had never heard any of these performers before. Our local radio stations never played them, or any music remotely that good. I listened every night, if I could. I never ordered any records from one of the principal sponsors, Randy's Record Shop in Gallatin, Tennessee. But I appreciated what I was hearing; I *loved* what I was hearing.

Did any of this act as a countervailing force to the steady diet of Jim Crow customs and stereotypes and dialect-based humor that surrounded me during these years? I honestly do not know. But I hope that it did. Maybe this music was at least some sort of antidote to the racial poison I absorbed every day. These men and women were fabulous performers, the music the best I had ever heard. I hope some of that got through to me in ways that transcended simply keeping time to the beat of those incredible songs.

If there was something I heard on WLAC that reinforced the

black stereotypes I had acquired over my ten or eleven or twelve years growing up in the South, it was probably the advertising. The products seemed to me to be aimed at an African American audience—Thunder Bolt Perfume, Bruton's Snuff, and White Rose Petroleum Jelly are the ones I remember. These would add an amusing note to my listening. But I hope any such thoughts were submerged in the sound of B. B. King's blues guitar. These wonderful musicians demonstrated, and I think in some ways I recognized, that black culture and black people were not confined to the likes of Ezekiel and Eneas Africanus and the preacher of "The Peasel Tree Sermon."

I could not continue my radio listening when I left for Woodberry Forest School in the fall of 1951. The rules were strict—nothing allowed after that final bell rang on the dorm every night. If you broke the rules, demerits would follow, and demerits had to be run off by going multiple times around a driveway circling much of the campus ("I ran a mile for a Camel" was a phrase we used regularly, although, fortunately, I had never started smoking and was uninterested in sneaking an illegal cigarette).

I am sorry to say that my time at Woodberry did nothing to break the hold of my Jim Crow upbringing. Indeed, almost everything surrounding me at the school reinforced it. All the masters were white. All the students were white, and almost all came from the South. Most of my "Rastus and Lulabelle" jokes I learned from my classmates there. When I went to visit friends' homes in places like Richmond, it was like going back to St. Pete: the help was black, the city was segregated.

There were many black men and women around the school, but they all had jobs in the kitchen or worked maintaining the grounds or served on the dorms in various menial ways. For example, once a week we put our dirty laundry in bags outside our dorm room for pickup and transportation to the school laundry. The African American man who worked on my dorm that first year was named Claude (I never learned his last name), and he would call out "Laundry day, laundry day!" every week when it rolled around. One boy on my dorm would mimic him when he did this. "Laundree day, Claude, laundree day!" he would yell, over and over again. I had been brought up never to consciously humiliate anyone, and I had no doubt that this was offensive behavior on this boy's part. But I never went so far as to call him on it. If I had, I am reasonably sure that someone, probably this boy, would have fired back, "What are you, Dew, some sort of nigger lover?" I was not willing to run that risk.

I mentioned earlier that every master at Woodberry had a nickname ("Red Cheese," "R.C.A.," "Brightmo Ghoul," "Uncle Mattie," the list was endless). Many of the African American workers had nicknames as well. I cannot recall many of these now, but I have never forgotten one.

The students served as waiters in the dining hall—useful training for the sons of privilege, I am sure was one reason. But we would pass in and out of the kitchen when we were waiting tables, and the work staff there was entirely black. One man in particular was a powerful individual, tall, muscular, with biceps that seemed as big as footballs to us. Whenever we had ice cream for dessert, he would scoop individual portions out of those frozen tubs as if he were lifting a cup of feathers. His nickname was "Super Nigger." I cannot recall ever saying that; I hope I did not. Dear's prohibition against the use of that word was absolute. I have an idea in the back of my mind that I shortened that supremely offensive nickname to "Supe"—not much of an act of courage on my part, but at least it allowed me to avoid using the tainted word. But I did not have the guts to challenge those who did.

All of this, from my infancy spent with *Ezekiel* through my three teenage years at Woodberry, all of this had trained me, once again, as a son of the South. But this training was different from my training as a Confederate youth. This training made me a racist, this training had real consequences, this training made me a part of the problem, *the* major problem of the South of my era: racial injustice on a massive scale, cradle-to-grave segregation. I had become a son of the Jim Crow South.

This was the heavy baggage, the unthinking baggage, I would be carrying north with me when I was seventeen and preparing to start my freshman year at Williams. Whether my white southern attitudes would survive my four years at a New England college was very much an open question at this point. Certainly nothing was predestined. Shucking that reptilian skin would not be easy.

3

The Unmaking of a Racist

I realized on my first day on the Williams campus in September 1954 that I had entered a new and, for me, very strange world. I had African American classmates, one of whom, Ted Wynne, I mentioned earlier. Ted and I were both residents of Entry F in Williams Hall, one of two big dorms in the freshman quad.

In the wake of my aborted "Rastus and Lulabelle" joke, I made it a point to speak to Ted. I could not bring myself to apologize; I was too embarrassed to do that. But I felt I had to talk to him, to let him know that I was willing to engage him in conversation just as I might do with any other member of my class. I cannot remember what we spoke about, but if Ted had heard me when I was telling that dialect joke, he did not let on. Much to my relief, we had a friendly conversation.

I realized as I walked away that something remarkable had just happened. I had never carried on anything approaching a real conversation with an African American individual—man, woman, or child—that even approached the level of the conversation I had just had, an exchange between equals. I was seventeen years old and had lived around black people all my life. But every previous conversation, literally every one, had been grounded in and restrained by the racial etiquette that governed exchanges between the races in my native South.

Ted Wynne and I became friends. He was from Worcester, Massachusetts, so we did not share a southern background, and it is fair to say that we did not become close friends. But we talked about what was going on at the college or in class or how the athletic teams were doing, and we were comfortable with each other. I know I was, and Ted gave every indication that he was, too. I have often thought to myself that my education, in some ways the most important part of my education, began at Williams well before I walked into my first classroom.

I have often wondered about my continuing acceptance of Jim Crow culture coexisting alongside the emerging reality of my life on a New England college campus. Was it simply the tenacious hold of my southern past or an exercise in bizarre compartmentalization? I simply cannot say. But I was simultaneously able to be friends with Ted and still walk into my sophomore American history class and cite Abraham Lincoln as my authority for defending racial segregation in the South. I could read about the brutal lynching of Emmett Till in Mississippi in the summer of 1955 and, a few short months later, write my comment about the whipping of John C. Calhoun's slave in Hofstadter's *American Political Tradition*. I wish I could explain this, but it mystifies me even now. My first two years at Williams were a roller coaster ride: defender of Jim Crow one moment, doubting Thomas the next. The grip of what Pop called "the basics" was a powerful one, but at least I was starting, slowly, to wake up during my freshman and sophomore years, still groggy, still half-asleep, but a process had begun. As I indicated earlier, it was often one or two steps forward followed by yet another move in the wrong direction, but the tectonic plates were starting to shift. I think that process of change and gradual transformation involved two things: consciousness raising and conscience raising.

My mother has a lot to do with the conscience-raising part of this equation. If there was one thing Dear tried to instill in my brother and me (besides good manners), it was to extend kindness and consideration to everyone with whom we came into contact, everyone, white or black. That is who she was, and I think it was instinctive on her part to try to instill those values in us as well. She led by example. As I mentioned before, within the paternalistic framework she embraced regarding race, this could make her a defender of Jim Crow, albeit a quiet one (certainly compared to my father), and an unthinking critic of the NAACP, while simultaneously feeling bad enough about Illinois and Joe's housing situation to take action to remedy it. If I had anything remotely approaching a conscience on matters regarding race, it was because of Dear.

The consciousness-raising dimension had both on-campus and off-campus aspects. At Williams, living with African American classmates, seeing them in class and in the big freshman dining hall, speaking with them on a fairly regular basis—these things constituted an unthinking, spontaneous challenge to my Jim Crow sensibilities. This casualness about race (indeed, forgetting totally about race more often than not) began to seem normal, natural, no big deal. In my native South, it would have been a very big deal. I also started to notice things when I left Williams.

One of my father's clients in St. Petersburg was the Seaboard Airline Railroad—"Through the Heart of the South" was the Seaboard's motto. Since Pop was technically a Seaboard employee, I could ride his pass on the crack streamliners, the Silver Meteor and the Silver Star, that ran from New York City to Florida.

I was returning home for Christmas in 1954 during my freshman year and had only been able to get a late seating in the dining car. All the waiters were African American, as were the cooks. I noticed as I was finishing my meal that all the patrons (we were all white) were seated at one end of the dining car. I did not think anything of it until one of the waiters drew a curtain across the middle of the car. At this point, African American passengers began to enter the car, all of whom were seated on the other side of the curtain.

I had been riding trains for years. Dear used to take John and me to Huntington regularly by rail. I loved trains (I still do), and I thought I knew just about everything there was to know about rail travel. But I had never noticed that Jim Crow curtain before. Then it hit me. Ted Wynne, my classmate, someone I considered a friend, could not be seated with me. He could not even enter the dining car until that curtain was closed. This is not right, I remember thinking, there is something wrong here. Looking back now, I think this was the first time I had directly questioned one of the Jim Crow folkways that I had grown up with, that I had taken for granted, that had been, to all intents and purposes, invisible to me before.

When I returned to campus after that Christmas, I started paying more attention, for the first time, to what was going on in the South in the wake of the *Brown* decision. I began reading the *New York Times,* and the *Times* had a succession of crack reporters covering events that would soon be boiling to the surface down there. My awareness was anything but acute, but I could not help noticing things like the start of the Montgomery bus boycott and the rise of Massive Resistance in Virginia. These things occurred in 1955 and 1956, and it was obvious that a struggle was under way, and very soon it was clear that my side of the color line was capable of some truly despicable acts.

My junior and senior years at Williams were the critical turning point for me. It was a combination of influences—becoming aware of events in the South as the civil rights battles unfolded, things that were happening on campus (including a life-changing seminar on the history of the Old South I took in the second semester of my junior year), and two absolutely critical occurrences that happened to me in the South—all taking place during my final two years of college. The collective impact of these events finally made me look fully into the face of bigotry and see it, clearly, unequivocally, and really for the first time, for the evil that it truly is.

Pop, our dog, Flip (named for my uncle), and me
in the side yard of our home, taken just before I left to board
the train for a trip back to Williams.

Strangely enough, it was the acquisition of my first automobile
that proved to be an important part of my change of heart. I spent
the summer between my sophomore and junior years at Williams
working at the Dew Motor Company in St. Petersburg. Uncle Roy
(I am sure at Pop's urging) had given me a job as a general facto-
tum around his Cadillac agency, doing everything from chatting
up new car customers until the real salesmen could take over to
sweeping out the shop floor in the service department first thing
in the morning before the mechanics got there.

During the summer, a "cream puff" (teenage lingo for a beautiful car back then) arrived as a trade-in on a new Cadillac—a 1955
Chevrolet Bel Air sedan, two-tone exterior (yellow and white),
turquoise interior. Less than a year old, almost no mileage, it was

beautiful, and quite naturally it caught my eye. I approached Pop tentatively about a possible purchase. It was available for $1,500, not an insignificant sum by any means, but I hoped it would be doable. I would contribute my summer savings if Pop would cover the balance. I would repay the loan out of any future earnings I came up with.

Pop had the idea that, if at all possible, students should not go into debt to pay for their college education. His two brothers had seen him all the way through UVa, and he never forgot what that had meant to him. I had gotten my act together at Williams, was making good grades, and had a shot at making Phi Beta Kappa my junior year. As a rising junior, I could keep a car on campus. So Pop made me an offer: keep working hard, focus on my academics (instead of road-tripping to nearby women's colleges all the time), and he would spring for the full cost. My joy knew no bounds. I would be driving back to school at the end of the summer in my own '55 Chevy, yellow and white, turquoise interior.

My trip north was carefully planned to minimize expenses: the first leg was to Orangeburg, South Carolina, where I could spend the night with my aunt Maude (my father's youngest sister) and Uncle Jimmy Albergotti, and their three children, my cousins Judy, Jimmy, and Bobby. On day two, I could drive to Woodberry and spend the night in one of the bunk beds in the alumni room at the gym. Day three would put me in Williamstown. It was that first day and night that would end up making an enormous difference in my life.

My route from St. Petersburg to Orangeburg took me through back roads, *really* back roads, of rural Florida, Georgia, and South Carolina. Uncle Jimmy had discovered after years of driving between Orangeburg and St. Pete that this very much off-the-beaten-path way was the best and most time-efficient route. He sent me a map; there were very few four-lane highways then, and no interstate system, and his route avoided the main north-south highway, US 301, which could be bumper-to-bumper traffic much of the time.

I had never been through places like Midway, Georgia, and Ridgeland, South Carolina, before—small towns I drove through on that first day. The rural poverty, the black poverty, I saw was stunning—children playing outside and whole families living in houses that had once apparently been slave cabins. The heat and humidity were oppressive, the fields scorching hot under the late August sun. Occasionally, I would pass a huge billboard reading "Impeach Earl Warren."

When I finally arrived in Orangeburg, I stopped downtown for a Pepsi (my usual, twelve ounces versus six in a Coke) to cool off a bit before going on to my aunt and uncle's house. As I entered the drugstore, I noticed a huge round decal on the glass front door reading "We Support the White Citizens' Council." It was Saturday afternoon, and downtown Orangeburg was crowded with black men, women, and children. A quick look around confirmed that every business establishment I could see from my vantage point was displaying that same oversized decal on a front door or plate glass window.

I asked Uncle Jimmy about what I had seen after dinner. The Citizens' Council had been formed in Indianola, Mississippi, in the summer of 1954 to oppose the *Brown* decision, and the organization many referred to as a "white-collar Klan" had spread like wildfire across the Deep South.[1] I did not know all that much about it, but I knew it was a white supremacist outfit from Mississippi and was probably the sort of thing Pop might have some sympathy with but would never join, in part because he never joined anything. Obviously, the White Citizens' Council had arrived in Orangeburg in a big way.

I admired Uncle Jimmy very much. He was a pediatrician, a very good one, I understood, and was smart, well spoken, well educated, and a thoroughly decent man. I knew he treated both white and black patients. His office was flanked by two waiting rooms, one for white, one for colored, but Uncle Jimmy's office was in the middle, and both races were welcome there where it really mattered. I was stunned when he told me he had joined the White Citizens' Council.

"Why, Uncle Jimmy?" I asked, and he could see I was dismayed. His answer rocked me back on my heels. "I had to, Charles," he replied. "I had to do it to protect my children." Uncle Jimmy made it clear to me that the ostracism, and probably worse, that would be visited on his daughter and his two sons was a price he did not feel he could pay. And he was absolutely certain there would be a price. He would be largely immune to any pressure the Citizens' Council could put on him; as the leading pediatrician in Orangeburg, he was too important. His children were another matter.

I understood the threat to his family; I could certainly put myself in my cousins' shoes and imagine the worst. But, I thought to myself as I headed north the next day, what's going on here? How can someone like Uncle Jimmy, a doctor, someone who has taken an oath to heal the sick, someone who treats both white and black patients, announce publicly that he considers probably half the children he sees to be something less than the white children he sees? They may have a darker skin, but those children (and their parents) come down with the same diseases, they need the same immunizations, black girls need to be told just like white girls to go to a friend's house and try to catch German measles before they reach puberty so they can acquire immunity and protect their babies from all sorts of terrible birth defects—I had heard Uncle Jimmy talk about all of these things.

I think now that this moment in Orangeburg was the equivalent of my witnessing Pop's out-of-control response to Bill's coming to the wrong door of our home. It was a searing experience: Uncle Jimmy Albergotti. In the White Citizens' Council. How can that be? Something was wrong, deeply wrong, with the society in which I had been brought up. I knew it. I could feel it in my gut. I almost felt sick when I got out on the road that next day.

The second thing that happened to me in the South was that I started talking, really talking, to Illinois. When I was home on vacation during my last two years of college, I began asking Dear to let me drive Illinois home on a regular basis. I wanted to have a chance to talk to her.

It probably took some steady nerves on Illinois's part to risk the trip home with me. My family drove year-old Cadillacs back then (Pop acquired Uncle Roy's personal demonstrator on a regular basis), and those huge machines, with no power brakes and no power steering, were a decided challenge for a teenage boy to handle. I knew when I was fifteen that I was going to have real trouble with my driver's test, so I practically memorized the state of Florida's driver's handbook; I figured that if I could ace the written part of the test, I might be able to cover the shortcomings that were bound to become manifest once I got behind the wheel. This turned out to be good thinking on my part. My grade of 100 on the written section of the exam, paired with the minimum passing score of 70 the state trooper gave me on the driving test, allowed me to pass by the proverbial skin of my teeth; trying to parallel park that big 1948 Cadillac sedan almost did me in. When we finished the driver's test, the trooper told me I would get my license, and then he got out of the car, stopped, turned, leaned in the open passenger-side window, and fixed me with a steady stare. His parting words were "Don't let this thing get away from you, kid."

Fortunately for me, Illinois was willing to trust me to get her safely to her house. I was older by then, a college student, for whatever that was worth, and we would get into the front seat of that big Cadillac and head for her home on the south side of town, a good twenty- or twenty-five-minute drive (Illinois took the segregated city bus to work).

She had already put in a full day's work by then, and she was inevitably tired, but I think she could tell that I wanted to talk about things, needed to talk about things, to discuss subjects we had never spoken about before. At this point, she had probably been working for my family for close to fifteen years.

I know it was that long because of something that happened when I was five or six years old and John was eight or nine. We got into a real fight, a knock-down, drag-out physical confrontation, over what God only knows. It happened in the backyard of our house, not far from the garage where Illinois was ironing. She heard us and came running out.

I should note here that Illinois's principal duties were to assist my mother in running our household—she cleaned the house weekly, she did the laundry, and on occasion she cooked for us, particularly her signature fried chicken, which Dear readily acknowledged was far superior to anything she could turn out along those lines. In no sense was Illinois hired as our nanny (or, to use the incredibly loaded term so rapturously employed by whites in the antebellum South, our "mammy"). Still, John and I knew that she was our mother's proxy when Dear was not around, and we did what she said. So when she yelled at us to stop fighting, we backed off. When we were far enough apart and reasonably calmed down, she gave us a stern talking-to. I shall never forget what she said at the end of this much-deserved dressing-down: "Brothers must be sweet." I am pretty sure John and I never had a battle like that again.

So I had known Illinois for a very long time and I had always respected her, but I actually knew very little about her until we started talking. As I recall, I broke the ice by asking her about her family and where she was from and why she and Joe moved to St. Petersburg; for some reason I knew they were not born in my hometown.

She told me that she had been born in a tiny town in the Florida Panhandle, Havana, just below the Georgia line, not far from the town of Quincy, Florida. Her maiden name was Browning, and she and Joe had settled in St. Pete in the hope that they could lead a better life than they could manage to do back home (I knew that area of the Panhandle was one of the poorest parts of the state). Their hopes had in many ways been realized, she told me. They had one child, a son, Roosevelt, who was several years older than I was, and she loved the home Pop and "Miss Dew," as she always called my mother, had helped them buy. It was clear that she had a genuine affection for the remarkable person I called Dear.

I am pretty sure it was her son's situation that gave me the occasion to raise the subject of race. Roosevelt had left St. Petersburg, moved to California, and landed a good job with one of the major airlines.

"I'm sorry he had to leave, Illinois," I remember saying, "but I understand why he did. There just aren't that many opportunities here," and I stopped before I said "for colored people." But she knew where I was going. I saw her glance in my direction.

"You know, Illinois, things have got to change down here," I went on. "It just isn't right that some people get treated unfairly just because of things like race."

"You're right, Charles," she responded, tentatively at first, but I think she could tell that I was on her side in this. "It's hard, it's just so hard sometimes."

Illinois and I were on the same honest page, and finally, after almost fifteen years, we were saying so.

In subsequent conversations, we began to discuss things more openly, and some of the ugly ways in which Jim Crow influenced her life came up.

"There is only one store where I can shop for a dress," she told me on one occasion. "All the stores will sell you one, but only Wilson-Chase will let colored folks try something on first." (I was silently proud at this moment that my Uncle Joe's furniture store was located there.)

She told me about where she and Joe had been living before they got their own place, and how they could never get the landlord (I recognized the name; it was on one of the department stores downtown where Illinois could not try on a dress) to do anything about the most basic repairs. I told her how glad I was she and Joe had gotten out of that place, although I was not brave enough to mention that Pop had argued before the city council that housing codes should not be toughened.

On one of our drives home after work, I raised the subject of the civil rights movement and the role Dr. Martin Luther King had been playing in Montgomery. She said how glad she was that people were doing something about the buses. She had to move to the rear when she rode the municipal transit system bus to work every morning, and I told her that was not right. "That's crazy," I think I said.

Dr. King's name came up in another way as well. My family had a new neighbor on the west side of our house, and these folks had acquired a large, black dog, some sort of Lab mix, I think, and they had named him Doc. Dear told me this, with a smile, and added that the dog was named for Dr. King but not as a compliment; the dog was named for Dr. King's color. I did not smile, but I did not say anything. No profile in courage for me on the home front yet. But Illinois and I agreed that this was tasteless in the extreme; neither one of us would use that name if the dog strayed into our yard.

I learned so much talking to Illinois, and just the talking was a lot of what I learned—just the fact that the two of us, both southerners, one black, one white, were having these conversations in the Jim Crow South. I even learned something about television quiz shows.

As I indicated earlier, Illinois cleaned the house for us every week, and when she reached the living room, Dear had no objection to her turning on the television, the only one we had in the house. If I was in the area, I would see what was on or pick up the audio, and it was almost always the same show. I soon figured out that Illinois timed her cleaning schedule so that she could reach the living room in time to watch *The Price Is Right.*

One day when we were driving to her house, I said, "Illinois, you seem to be a big fan of Bill Cullen and *The Price Is Right*—it must be your favorite show."

"I do like that show, and I like Bill Cullen," she replied. "And you know, Charles, it is the only show that ever has colored people on as guests."

I had no idea. This, I thought, is the sort of humiliation that she has to put up with every day of her life.

One of our conversations stands out in my memory above all the others. In the course of this particular drive home, she said something so profound, so on target, that it has stuck with me vividly all these years. I do not remember the exact context; I think we may have been talking about how those insane Jim Crow customs had grown up in the first place and why they seemed so intractable. But I remember exactly what Illinois said, and I remember that she spoke with genuine anguish. She seemed to be on the verge of tears. Her flash of insight came in the form of a question she put to me:

"Charles, why do the grown-ups put so much hate in the children?"

My conversations with Illinois while I was home during my last two years of college were probably the most important step I took along the path that led ultimately to my unmaking as a racist. Looking back, I think that they were more important than anything else that I did, or read about, or studied in class, or watched on television.

I know there is a risk that my description of our conversations may seem like a tired cliché, something scripted from recent novels describing the enlightenment that comes when bigoted but well-meaning white folks receive an education at the hands of long-time African American employees. But these conversations across the color line did happen—at least they happened to me, and I suspect I was not alone in this regard. Clichés seem to come into being for a reason.

I did not mention our discussions to Dear, and I certainly did not tell Pop about them. It might well have put Illinois's job at risk if I had, although I find it difficult to believe that Dear would have fired Illinois under any circumstances. But Illinois and I had reached a new place in our long acquaintance with each other. I hope our talks on these drives home after work did something positive for her. For me, they were of immeasurable importance in helping me break free from the racism I had acquired in my first seventeen years growing up in the Jim Crow South.

Like my conversations with Illinois, the national news increasingly confirmed my growing doubts about Jim Crow. Fred Rudolph had told me when I was a sophomore that I should be up on the stage with that South Carolina editor who was defending segregation. He would not have said that to me during my junior and senior years. Slowly but surely, I was changing. I distinctly recall watching television news coverage of the Little Rock school crisis in September 1957. I remember my reaction to the ugly, distorted faces of the white men and women in that mob outside Central High School, screaming at the well-dressed African American children trying to go to class. The people in that mob disgusted me. I did not want to be like them. I did not want anything to do with people like that. I, we, the South, surely we were better than that.

I was nearing a decisive breaking point with my white southern culture, but I had yet to come out of the closet, as it were, at my own home. Two events that took place at Williams College during my senior year finally led me to make that break—my profile in courage, finally, on the Dew home front. And that break precipitated a family crisis that made me take stock of my actions in a way I never anticipated.

Oddly enough, both events at Williams centered on my membership in a fraternity.

Fraternities dominated social life at my all-male college back then, and I joined the Delta Psi house—St. Anthony Hall as it was generally called—at the beginning of my sophomore year. My class, the class of 1958, was one of the first to delay rushing past the start of the freshman year, and I had plenty of time to size up the fraternity scene and decide where I wanted to land.

My father had been in the Phi Delta Theta fraternity at UVa, and John had joined the Phi Delts at Williams in part because of that, I suspect. His house had run afoul of the national fraternity, however. The Williams chapter had pledged a Jewish student in John's class and had been summarily expelled from the national; John's house was now strictly a local fraternity, Phi Delta, and John had discouraged me from joining, although he had many good friends there whom I liked very much.

St. Anthony Hall proved to be a good choice for me—nice guys, including some Jewish students, and many of my closest friends, but no African American members. Black students were not all that numerous at Williams then, but those who wished to join fraternities seemed to be able to join one—Ted Wynne was an officer in the Sigma Phi house and ran their rush very successfully. I was elected to serve as house president my senior year and got ready to run the rush for the St. A.'s.

That rush season provided a scene I can remember as vividly as if it were yesterday. The fraternities had come up with a system we called "Total Opportunity," which was designed to make sure that all the sophomores who wanted to join a fraternity received a bid. Those who fell through the cracks the first round without a single bid would be picked up; the house presidents would be given the names, we would take the list back to our respective houses for consideration, and then we would reassemble, with each house taking one student as we went around the table until everyone had a bid.[2]

Our sophomore pledge class could not understand why one of their classmates had been passed over on the first round—sure, he was Jewish, and he had not gone to prep school, but he was a great guy, fabulous sense of humor, amid a number of other accolades.

When I knocked on the door to his room in the Berkshire Quad (sophomore housing back then), I felt like I had come as a prince bearing a marvelous gift. He opened the door, and he stepped into the hall so his roommates would not overhear our conversation. As I explained that I was there to extend him a bid, that his fellow classmates were enthusiastic about his joining the house, that *all* of us were enthusiastic about his joining the house, and that we *really* wanted him to do so, I saw a half smile form on his face and he glanced to the side, as I later thought, to avoid laughing out loud. He knew this was a charade. He had been passed over completely in the first round, and here I was telling him we were head over heels to make him a brother. But he graciously accepted my offer, we shook hands, and I left.

As I walked back to my house, my princely feelings of noblesse oblige had turned to ashes in my mouth. "What in the hell are we doing to each other?" I remember thinking. "No one should have to go through what this student has just had to endure." The entire selection process suddenly struck me as humiliating in the extreme. I did not make the jump immediately to see the parallels to the humiliation inflicted daily on African Americans in the Jim Crow South, but I was only one step away from that recognition. It came in the spring of my senior year.

The national Delta Psi officers were visiting, all adult men, and the national president was a Virginian, from Richmond. Since I was a Woodberry boy and he was a St. A. from the UVa chapter, he assumed he could speak frankly to me, and he drew me aside for a private conversation. "Charles, I hope the house here will have the good sense never to pledge a nigger," he said to me. I felt a knot form in the pit of my stomach and was flooded with a sense of anger and disgust. I had been taught since infancy to be polite around adults. But all that training meant nothing to me at that moment. I turned on my heels without saying a word and left the room.

I had finally broken free, really, totally free. Something had snapped in my education as a southerner, in my education as a racist. I had reached a new place, intellectually, culturally, perhaps even spiritually. I was a different person from that Confederate youth, the born and bred southern white boy, the unthinking bigot who had stepped onto the Williams campus as a seventeen-year-old four years earlier.

I see looking back that my first step was to get out of the South. I am absolutely convinced that if I had not done so, I would not have been able to break free from the poisonous racism I had absorbed growing up. I certainly would not have done so while I was in college. I would not have had an African American classmate in my freshman dorm, an African American friend, an African American with whom I could hold a normal conversation. I would have had no context in which to judge that curtain being drawn in the dining car on the Silver Meteor. I am reasonably certain it never would have occurred to me to open the pages of the *New York Times* if I had been on the campus of a southern college or university. I probably would not have had the reaction I had driving through poverty-stricken parts of the rural South, having seen for myself how at least some of the other half were forced to live. I am reasonably sure I would not have heard Uncle Jimmy tell me he had to join the White Citizens' Council. I probably would never have even approached an honest conversation with Illinois. And I know I would not have had a teacher like Professor Robert C.

L. Scott, who did as much to influence the course of the rest of my life as anyone.

Bob Scott was a native of Minnesota, but he knew the South well. His father was an officer in the United States Army—the last general to command the horse cavalry—and, like most Army brats, Bob had spent a lot of time in the South when he was growing up. Maybe this gave him some understanding of the culture shock I was going through as I landed on the Williams College campus. Maybe the fact that his great-grandfather was a major in the Fourth Alabama Regiment had something to do with it. Or maybe Bob Scott was just a great teacher. But whatever the reason may be, he took me under his wing while I was a Williams student.[3]

It was largely because of Bob that I decided to become a history major. He agreed to serve as my adviser, and when it came time to think about doing honors work, he strongly encouraged me to write a thesis. My first step in that direction was to enroll in Bob's honors seminar on the history of the Old South. This class, taken in the second semester of my junior year, was one of the things I experienced at Williams that changed my life.

My Old South seminar was a revelation to me. My *Youth's Confederate Primer* was not the last word, or even the first word, on anything. We read great historians like David M. Potter, Kenneth M. Stampp, and C. Vann Woodward. We studied slavery, antebellum politics, rising sectional tension, secession, and the Confederacy—all with the gloves off. I read the antebellum pro-slavery defenders, leading intellectuals in the Old South, like my ancestor Thomas Roderick Dew, who was writing the same stuff in the 1830s that I was being brought up on in the 1950s.

Professor Scott, as I called him then (we later became colleagues when I joined the faculty at Williams in 1977), did not preach to me or to any of us in the seminar. He did not have to. The materials we were reading spoke for themselves. It may not sound like much—to have the myths about slavery, the Old South, and the Confederacy that I had absorbed over the course of my life blown out of the water. But believe me, this part of my education was very, very important to me. I was thinking about my part of the country in ways that had never occurred to me before, critically, analytically, with a mounting need to know and understand. I could not wait to get to class. Halfway through the seminar, I wanted to be a historian. I would be applying to graduate school in history, not headed to UVa law school like my brother.

When it came time to settle on an honors thesis topic, I looked south—no surprise there. I had expressed an interest in the period known as the New South, the post-Reconstruction South, the years when my ancestors tried to turn things around after the trauma of war and defeat (my Tennessee grandfather, Givens Dew, born in 1866, was part of that generation). C. Vann Woodward's magisterial *Origins of the New South, 1877–1913* was my bible.[4] I decided, with Professor Scott's help, to focus on the politics of two Upper South states, Tennessee and Virginia, in the decade of the 1870s. I was so anxious to get a head start on my thesis research that I enrolled in a summer school history course (on Reconstruction) at the University of Florida in Gainesville in order to gain access to a first-class university library in the South.

Professor Scott was on leave during my senior year at Williams, but I had a superb younger historian waiting in the wings: Jack Sproat, a recent PhD from the University of California at Berkeley and a student of one of my emerging galaxy of American historians, Kenneth M. Stampp. Jack guided me through that year with a superb blend of enthusiasm and tough love. My thesis, carrying the cumbersome title of "Whiggery and Redemption in the Upper South: Post-Reconstruction Politics in Tennessee and Virginia in the 1870's," began to take shape.

(This is jumping ahead a bit, but one of the history department readers for my thesis turned out to be Fred Rudolph. I still treasure his assessment of my work after I submitted my final draft shortly before graduation. "A straight forward account adhering to responsible canons of historical scholarship," he wrote. "I liked reading a thesis in which the *narrative* was not warped and the interpretation not stretched to fit the warped narrative."[5] I had managed to climb down from that stage where Fred had placed me alongside the segregationist editor back when I was a sophomore. Maybe I could make it in the real world as a historian after all.)

By the time I took Bob Scott's class and settled on my thesis topic, both in the spring semester of my junior year, I was already questioning a great deal of what I had grown up with as a son of the Jim Crow South. My education, and my Old South seminar in particular, had deepened my doubts dramatically about "the basics" (as Pop referred to my supposedly impregnable southern values). I felt intellectually exhilarated. Increasingly, I felt culturally liberated. I felt that I was finally managing to shuck that reptilian skin of racism that had wrapped itself around me as a white southerner. But what I was learning and experiencing at Williams was making my father increasingly angry.

For years, we had had a habit of gathering as a family in the sunroom after dinner to talk. I very much looked forward to these occasions when I was home from school on holidays. It was a way to reconnect with my family, to find out what had been going on while I was away. But these after-dinner conversations became increasingly fraught. I started questioning some of Pop's more outrageous statements. If he had been drinking, which was often the case, he would launch into extended jeremiads about liberals and blacks, and he sometimes expanded his list of culprits to include Jews and Catholics as well. If I pushed back, which I started doing, he would get even angrier.

The breaking point came during spring vacation of my senior year at Williams. It was March 1958. After one of Pop's particularly bitter tirades against the *Brown* decision (as far as Pop was concerned, that old bone was never too tired to chew on), I blurted out that he was dead wrong about that. "The *Brown* decision is clearly supported by the equal protection clause of the Fourteenth Amendment, Pop," I almost shouted—I was fed up with listening to this stuff. "I think I know more about American constitutional history than you do!" He went silent after I said this, and we spoke very little before I left for school shortly thereafter.

I had been back at Williams for only a few days when Dear called. She told me Pop was hurt and angry over what I had said, that she had never seen him so bitter and upset. She pleaded with me to call and apologize to him.

To repeat, I was in the second semester of my final year of college. I had been speaking openly with Illinois for over a year by then. I had seen those grotesque white faces at Little Rock. I had had my "Total Opportunity" moment with that sophomore student (who turned out to be one of the finest individuals I had the privilege of knowing during my four years at Williams). I had turned my back on the national fraternity president when he assumed I was his racist comrade in arms. I had chucked my Confederate youth into the dustbin of history. And I had finally, finally, managed to break loose from my racist moorings. The last thing in the world I wanted to do was to apologize to my father for challenging what I increasingly saw as bigoted, racist, and irrational positions which only seemed to be getting worse with time.

I was also feeling my oats, and more than just a little bit. My dream of studying southern history in graduate school was becoming a reality. I had recently won a Woodrow Wilson Fellowship that would cover almost all the cost of my multiyear quest for a PhD. I had been admitted to the Johns Hopkins University in Baltimore, the school at the top of my list because C. Vann Woodward, the preeminent southern historian in the country, taught there and had agreed to take me on as one of his students.

But Dear's call had hit me hard. She had sounded anxious, even desperate, to patch up the rift between my father and me.

I literally sat down to think; I can remember doing this and what went through my mind—anger, frustration (probably some unrecognized father-son rivalry), a sense that I should stick to my guns since I had finally decided to open fire at home on what I saw as my father's—the South's—rank ignorance and bigotry. But I realized that I had to make a choice. I could hold fast to my position, and my anger, and widen the breach. Or I could try to close it.

As I thought about things, I came to realize something that, in retrospect, I am very glad occurred to me in that signal moment. No matter his faults and his prejudices, I loved my father, very much. I could get extremely angry with him, but he was, in many ways, a wonderful man, and he had been a terrific father in almost every respect. He had his flaws, certainly, and they were not trivial. But I loved him. And I loved Dear. I decided to make that call.

Pop did not say a whole lot when we spoke, but he did accept my apology, and it was clear that he was glad that I had called. The air had been cleared. Dear heaved a great sigh of relief, she told me later. She had been doing a lot of praying, and she felt that her prayers had been answered.

I knew in the future that I would have to stay out of discussions with Pop about politics and race. He was not about to change his ideas about such matters, and I was not about to change mine. Bringing up contentious issues would only trigger another outburst and poison the atmosphere at home once again. I suspect that he reached the same conclusion because he did not try to goad me into arguments. We would have to find alternatives for those discussions in the sunroom and around the dining room table, moments that I used to take such pleasure in.

And we did find alternatives. There was family, of course, and his law practice, and the changing nature of St. Petersburg as the population grew and the city expanded and the economy diversified. But more than anything, we settled on that old southern staple, football. A lot of talk about football. Woodberry Forest football. Williams College football. University of Florida football. University of Miami football. Professional football. It mattered not.

My father had become an avid Baltimore Colts fan for some reason (which made my decision to go to Johns Hopkins instead of UVa law school much more palatable to him), and the Colts were on a roll in those days: Johnny Unitas, Lenny Moore, Ray Berry and company, and the "Greatest Game Ever Played"—the Colts' December 1958 overtime championship win against the New York Giants.

My father and I got so excited during that game that we pulled out all the stops in our effort to secure a victory. Our lumbering basset hound, Rascal, had wandered into the living room just as the game turned in the Colts' favor, and I was tasked with the job of petting him continuously so that he would stay in the room to ensure that the Colts' luck would hold. Pop got so excited during the Colts' final drive that he managed to break one of the runners on his rocking chair as he used an amazing wrench of body language to get the Colt fullback, Alan Ameche, over the goal line for the winning touchdown.

So we talked a lot about football, and we watched a lot of football, and we managed to fill the time when I was at home. And I am very glad that we did. My father died much too young. He was only seventy-two when the end came in 1975. He was suffering from a variety of maladies, but the principal villain was leukemia. Pop wanted me in the hospital room with him on that last night, and I was there. I have never been sorry that I decided to back away from that confrontation during my last year of college. It was one of the wisest decisions I ever made, and I am grateful now that I had enough sense when I was twenty-one years old to make it.

Dear stayed on in our home at 234 Twenty-Fifth Avenue

North, and Illinois stayed on as well, working for my mother for a number of years after Pop died. But Illinois's health was also failing. As Dear told me after Illinois died, she had suffered from high blood pressure for years and had, Dear thought, been lax about taking her medication. My mother's voice carried an unmistakable note of grief as she told me this. Dear had added enough to cover the cost of her prescriptions to what she paid Illinois every week, but my mother was afraid that money was being spent elsewhere. It was obvious that Illinois's death had hit Dear hard; it saddened me enormously as well. She had been a "faithful soul," as Dear put it. Those words would seem to resemble far too closely the "faithful darkie" stereotype mentioned earlier, but it was clear to me when my mother said them that her words carried genuine respect and love, not condescension. For me, Illinois had become a friend, someone I could talk to honestly and openly, someone who had taken the time at the end of her long workday to offer me a lifeline that had helped pull me out of the swamp of racial prejudice. I find it hard to put into words the gratitude I feel for her.

Dear, too, moved beyond her acceptance of the Jim Crow ethos after Pop died. We opened up our conversations, and she admitted that she had been largely blind to the injustices that had been inflicted on African Americans for far too long. She came to see the civil rights movement as a necessary corrective to a historic wrong, to generations of historic wrongs.

Dear never sought to replace Illinois. I think my mother considered her *sui generis* and was unwilling to take on anyone else full-time. The only people who worked regularly in the house after Illinois died were the home care providers who came on board when Dear started showing serious symptoms of Parkinson's disease. My mother's death came in 1991 when she was eighty-six years old. And as had been the case with Pop, I was able to spend some wonderful days with her shortly before she died.

After all that I have said about my white southern upbringing, it may come as a surprise to some that I credit Dear and Pop with helping me recover from the cultural and spiritual disease I contracted in my youth, for that is what racism is, a disease. Yes, they were present at the creation of my Confederate youth and, more importantly, my unthinking acceptance of the color line. But they also, I believe, provided me with at least some of the tools I needed to reject my Jim Crow past.

Dear gave me a basic sense of fairness, of concern, of kindness, even a belief in the essential goodness of the vast majority of mankind. That is who she was, and I think my brother and I share some of those same qualities. As I wrote earlier, my sense of right and wrong, in essence my conscience, rests in large part on the humanistic moral foundation she laid down for me.

And I think Pop imparted something that was of vital assistance to me as well. It was because of him that I attended Williams, of course, but that was not all. Pop believed in personal honesty and integrity above everything else. It was essentially the old adage "To thine own self be true." I remember him telling me something when I was still quite young that has stayed with me all these years.

"People have to be able to trust me completely, Charles," he said. "Nothing is more important to me than my integrity. If I lose that, I've lost everything. I would have to stop practicing law." I know my father and I came to profoundly different definitions of the meaning of "integrity" when applied to matters of race and the creation of a more humane politics and what constitutes social justice. But I would like to think that his words helped me when it came time for me to face the worst of my native South, when it came time for me to redefine my own sense of integrity and what it meant to lead an honest existence.

The embrace of Jim Crow as a way of life and a system of beliefs for white southerners was powerful and seductive. White supremacy is a noxious weed that plants deep roots. I know this firsthand. But I also know that racism can be overcome. I think the best of my mother and father helped me pull those racist weeds up by the roots and cast them as far away from me as I possibly could. In the end, despite everything that had gone before, my parents helped me bend the arc of my own moral universe, my personal moral universe, toward justice.

4

The Document

We beg leave to give you the state of our Negro Market....

An academic life is inherently lacking in high drama. It is a highly individualistic enterprise for most of us, intellectually exciting, certainly, but absent those gripping moments that seem to occur in a number of other professions. Much of what historians do, we do at our desks or in those quiet archives. No spectacular diagnoses are made, no operating room miracles are performed, no towering skyscrapers rise from our drafting tables, no court cases are won by an unexpected flourish of lawyerly legerdemain. We research and we read and we try not to let the desire for perfection—writer's block, it is usually called—stop us cold and keep us from writing what, we hope, is at least very good history.

And then, if we are fortunate enough to hold the fruits of our largely solitary labors in our hands one day, we often look at that book that took so much out of us (and often our families) and say, "Is that all there is to show for all that blood, sweat, and tears?" And when the reviews come in (unless, of course, our precious volume is totally ignored), we focus obsessively on the most trivial words of criticism and ignore even the most lavish praise.

Assessing our teaching is, in some ways, even more difficult. Yes, we can count the numbers in our classes, we can try to read the students' attention levels, we can do our best to deliver clear lectures and to run brisk discussions, we can grade their papers and exams, and we can leave class with a mild sense of satisfaction or, more likely, an acute sense of "Damn, I can teach better than that!"

A friend from my early teaching days summed up this sense of classroom frustration beautifully. He was an Episcopal chaplain at Louisiana State University in Baton Rouge, and one day he told me something that has stuck with me all these years.

"You know something, Charles," he said, "you and I are in the same business."

"How is that?" I asked.

"We are both up there preaching a gospel and we really don't know if we are saving any souls or not," he replied. So true.

But every now and then, a rumble of thunder rolls across our normally placid scholarly sky. Something happens that startles us, forces us to take immediate notice, even makes us stop in our tracks and reexamine what we have been doing as historians trying to unravel the past. I have not experienced many of these moments, but they have occurred. Two of these bolts from the blue are at the core of this book.

I had been invited by a good friend and very fine historian, Phil Schwarz, to speak at a summer conference on slavery he had organized for public school teachers. This was shortly after I had published my second book, *Bond of Iron: Master and Slave at Buffalo Forge,* and the setting for this conference could not have been better: Robert E. Lee's ancestral home at Stratford Hall in Tidewater Virginia. High school and middle school teachers, both white and black, from all over the country were in attendance.

Bond of Iron focused on a group of slave ironworkers and their owner, a man named William Weaver, and Buffalo Forge, his iron-making enterprise located in the Valley of Virginia, not far from the town of Lexington. The records I had discovered over many years spent doing research on this project were remarkable. I was able to carry my investigation of these industrial slave workers and their families down to the individual level. I could trace their work over a period of years, their earnings (they were paid in cash or goods for exceeding their daily or weekly tasks), and their expenditures (incredibly valuable information for studying slave life); document their marriages, the births, and too often the deaths, of their children; and describe both their unavoidable accommodation to their enslavement and their brave resistance to their bondage. I had come to admire these men and women tremendously, and I tried to tell their story as fully and faithfully as I could in my allotted time at Stratford Hall. I brought with me Xerox copies of some amazing documents to help illustrate my points, and I wove them into my comments as I went along. I finished satisfied that I had told my story reasonably well; I had given my assignment—to say something meaningful about industrial slavery—a decent shot.

When I opened the floor for discussion, the first hand that went up belonged to an African American man.

"How did someone as white as you come to study our history?" he asked.

Now there is no question that I favor the Scots side of my ancestry—fair complexion (and far too much sun exposure during my youth in Florida), light-colored eyes, and a truly strange mix of hair, some residual blond from my younger days and gray from my more advanced years. So I definitely am, and certainly look like, a white guy. No issue taken there. It was the heart of his question that rocked me back on my heels.

So why had I, a southern white boy born and bred (I still have a slight accent, particularly if I am speaking in the South), come to study black history? Yes, I had been liberated, as it were, during my college years, but still, why? What had prompted me to devote all those years to trying to uncover the story of Sam and Nancy Williams, Henry and Ann Towles, Garland and Dicey Thompson, Tooler, Harry Hunt Jr., Henry Matthews, and the other men and women of the Buffalo Forge slave community?

I was struck dumb by his question. I did not have a clue how to answer.

If there is one thing we learn as classroom teachers, it is that on far too many occasions we have to be quick on our feet, display a nimble move or two, indulge in a little verbal two-step to cover the fact that we have absolutely no idea how to answer a question a student has just posed. Our best tack when this happens is invariably to avoid the question and revert to something we do know.

A bit of flashback is necessary here, so I ask the reader to keep that teacher's question in mind as I fill in some necessary autobiographical detail.

At Johns Hopkins, I settled on a dissertation topic that would combine my growing fascination with the antebellum, Civil War, and Reconstruction South with my passion for archival research. I discovered the latter when, as a Hopkins student, a bunch of us regularly made the trek to Washington so that we could work on our papers for Vann Woodward's research seminar. From nearby Baltimore, we had ready access to the mecca of all archival depositories, the Manuscript Reading Room of the Library of Congress. It was there that I found out that I was what is known in the historian's trade as an "archives rat." I suspect that phrase needs no explanation.

Professor Woodward returned from a conference in Richmond at one point with news that the records of the Tredegar Iron Works in that city had just become available for research at the Virginia State Library (now the Library of Virginia). I knew the Tredegar by reputation: the premier manufacturing facility in the antebellum and Civil War South, the source for the armor plate for the *Merrimack* and other Confederate ironclads, the manufacturer of untold ordnance for the Confederate military and railroad iron for civilian use. So I drove down to Richmond in my '55 Chevy, took a room for a week at the YMCA (the only place I could afford on a graduate school budget), and dug into the Tredegar records.

I was hooked after the first day. The collection was amazing. The Tredegar and the ambitious, hard-driving Virginia entrepreneur who built this astonishing southern enterprise, Joseph Reid Anderson, became the focus of my doctoral dissertation.

After I finished my field exams at Hopkins in 1961, I moved to Richmond to work on the massive Tredegar collection. I took a small basement apartment on Franklin Street, and my daily walk to the library took me past locations that, although I did not know it at the time, were the streets and neighborhoods where Richmond's slave traders, slave jails, and slave auction houses were once clustered, places that will figure largely in subsequent chapters of this book.

By the time I finished and revised my dissertation, hoping to find a publisher, I was teaching southern history at LSU and Vann Woodward had relocated to Yale. He graciously recommended my manuscript to the Yale University Press, and it came out under that imprint in 1966 as *Ironmaker to the Confederacy: Joseph R. Anderson and the Tredegar Iron Works.* So this is where I went in my mind—to the sprawling Tredegar Iron Works on the banks of the James River in Richmond, Virginia—when that inquisitive teacher at Stratford Hall blindsided me with his question.

"You know," I blurted out after too long a pause, "when I was working on my dissertation on the Tredegar, there were slave workers there in substantial numbers, but I wasn't able to learn very much about them. The Tredegar records are incredibly rich but not on this phase of their operations. So I decided I wanted to focus my next project on slave ironworkers, and I started to look for archives where good records might exist." I was dancing as fast as I could.

And then I stopped dead. I knew this was not what this teacher wanted to know. I paused again, but this time actually to think.

"I'm not really answering your question, am I?" I said. "To tell you the truth, I never really sat down and thought about this before. I just went after what fascinated me as a historian. But I think I started studying the South and race and slavery because I wanted to know how white southerners—my people—had managed to look evil in the face every day and not see what was right there in front of them, in front of us." I had never put this thought into words before. "I grew up in the Jim Crow South," I went on to say. "Segregation was all around me. I never saw it. My ancestors participated in slavery; one of them wrote an elaborate defense of slavery. How did they manage to do this? Why couldn't we see this evil? It was right there in front of us. Every day. Slavery in the nineteenth century. Segregation in mine. Moral abominations. Yet we were oblivious to all of it."

My questioner seemed satisfied with this, perhaps even a little taken aback by the unmistakable note of passion that crept into my voice as I tried to put all of this into words. I spent the rest of my allotted time on the program answering questions, but I cannot recall a single thing I was asked, or how I replied. I was still fixated on his question and the much larger and much more important question I had raised myself in response to his query. I am not exaggerating in the slightest when I say that his question and my response have been with me ever since. It is essentially the question, once again, that I posed at the conclusion to the first chapter of this book and have been silently repeating in one form or another on practically every page: "How had I, we, all of us white southerners become such unthinking racists to begin with?"

The shock of recognition about why I, as a historian, had become so intently focused on race and slavery—essentially as a way to come to grips with the role of race and segregation, the color line, in my own life—was brought home to me a second, and equally powerful, time when another of those intermittent thunderclaps suddenly and unexpectedly rocked my normally quiet scholarly life. And this one, like some of those powerful moments from my younger days, occurred on the Williams College campus.

Some essential background once again needs to be added here, so please bear with me.

In 1965, my academic travels had taken me to LSU, and it was in Louisiana that I met Robb Reavill Forman on a blind date. A friend of mine in the English department, Miller Williams, was working on the poetry of Robb's grandfather, John Crowe Ransom, and Miller took pity on me as an unattached bachelor and set the two of us up on a date. Robb was living in New Orleans at that time, and I drove down for what turned out to be a wonderful evening. We started dating regularly—New Orleans was (and I am sure still is) an amazing place to conduct a courtship—and we were married in January 1968 in the Episcopal Chapel at LSU. During the course of that year, the University of Missouri at Columbia offered me a job teaching southern history, and we decided to make the move.

Robb and I bought a house in Columbia and settled in for what we thought in all probability would be our home for the foreseeable future. We had not been in our new house very long before we read an article in the local paper that stunned us. A man named George McElroy, an African American high school teacher from Houston, was bunking with the university's football team because he could not find a room to rent in Columbia. He had won a *Wall Street Journal* scholarship, and had come to Missouri to work on his MA in journalism, but whenever he knocked on the door of someone advertising a room for rent, the room had miraculously just been taken. He had in the past helped recruit some very fine football players from his high school for the Missouri squad and had taken up temporary quarters there. Obviously, he was being systematically Jim Crowed out of a room all over town. Robb and I were appalled. We called the athletic office and told them we had a spare bedroom Mr. McElroy was welcome to occupy for as long as he wished. George McElroy took us up on our offer, and we had the good fortune of having a truly remarkable man become a part of our lives that year. He finished his MA, went back to Houston, and subsequently became an award-winning columnist for the *Houston Post*. Robb and I gained a friend that year, someone who helped both of us get over whatever residual awkwardness in the presence of African Americans we might have retained from our years growing up in the Jim Crow South.

Our expectation that we would probably be in Columbia for the duration turned out to be premature. Two invitations for me to serve as a visiting faculty member came along—the first to the University of Virginia in Charlottesville in 1970–71 and then to Williams College for the 1977–78 academic year.

Both turned out to be memorable. It was in Charlottesville that our first child, our son Charles Stephen Dew, was born, and our second boy, John Forman Dew (aka Jack, after my father and Robb's uncle, Jack Ransom), was born in 1973 after we returned to Columbia. Then in 1977, Williams College came along with an invitation to come for a year as a visiting professor of history. When Williams subsequently invited me to stay on as a regular faculty member, our fate was sealed. We made what has turned out to be our last move, and it was a collective decision. The boys loved Williamstown, as did Robb. Her writing career had just begun to take off, and Williamstown offered her what she most needed—a quiet place to think and write and a community that would respect her need for privacy when she was working.

So it was at Williams, far from my native South, that that second scholarly thunderclap occurred.

I remember vividly the day Bob Volz, custodian of the Chapin Library, the extraordinary rare book and manuscript collection at Williams College, invited me over to see a new acquisition. When I held this document in my hand, I knew I was holding one of those sources I described at the beginning of this book, an example of the "stuff of history" that, once seen, is impossible to forget. This single sheet of paper communicated something of profound and fundamental importance to me about the South. It has influenced my understanding of southern history in ways that are visceral as well as intellectual. And given my background as a white southerner, it resonated in deeply personal ways that I find difficult to put into words.

When being introduced to someone for the first time in the South, it is not uncommon to be asked, "Now, who are your people?" Well, here they were. My people, my side of the slave/ free divide, had generated this document. Not my direct ancestors, but my people nonetheless. Antebellum Virginians I might have been fighting alongside had I been in those Rapidan River trenches—perhaps in that same stretch that today stands near Woodberry Forest School—during the last months of the Civil War. Given where I was born and raised and what I believed back in 1954 when I was seventeen and walking those same trenches, I am sure that spot, or one very much like it, is exactly where I would have been standing had I been living in Virginia in the spring of 1865.

The manuscript that prompted these thoughts is a printed broadside, with space left open for filling in vital information by hand. I have read it countless times over the years, and it has yet to lose any of the gut-wrenching power it had on first reading. I begin my courses on the Old South and the American Civil War by passing out copies at the opening meeting of the class. I ask my students to read it and tell me what they see. Their reaction is often one of puzzlement followed by stunned disbelief, as well it should be at the onset of the twenty-first century. But then the ramifications of what they are looking at begin to sink in. It is a profoundly educational document. And it prompted me to re- search and write this book.

Betts & Gregory,
AUCTIONEERS,
Franklin Street,
RICHMOND, VA.

Richmond, August 2 1860.

Dear Sir:

We beg leave to give you the state of our Negro Market, and quote them as follows:

Extra Men, - - - - -	$ *1550*	to $ *1625*
No. 1 do. - - - - -	$ *1450*	to $ *1550*
Second rate or Ordinary do. - -	$ *1100*	to $ *1250*
Extra Girls, - - - - -	$ *1375*	to $ *1450*
No. 1 do. - - - - -	$ *1300*	to $ *1350*
Second rate or Ordinary do. - -	$ *900*	to $ *1100*
Boys 4 feet high, - - - -	$ *500*	to $ *600*
Boys 4 feet 3 inches high, - - -	$ *600*	to $ *700*
Boys 4 feet 6 inches high, - - -	$ *800*	to $ *900*
Boys 4 feet 9 inches high, - - -	$ *1000*	to $ *1100*
Boys 5 feet high, - - - -	$ *1100*	to $ *1250*

Girls of same height of boys about the same prices.

Good young woman & first child $1300 to $1450

The Market is dull this week owing to the fact that there are but few Southern buyers in the market.

Yours Respy,
Betts & Gregory

Price circular issued by Betts & Gregory, Richmond auctioneers, containing market guidance and showing a range of prices for multiple categories of slave men, women, and children, dated August 2, 1860. (Chapin Library, Williams College, Williamstown, Mass.; Class of 1940 Americana Fund)

This broadside, dated August 2, 1860, is a market report—a list of prices current—prepared by the slave-trading firm of Betts & Gregory, Auctioneers, Franklin Street, Richmond, Virginia.[1]

I think this document hit me so hard because it represented, on a single page, the embodiment of the evil that was slavery. It spoke, more powerfully than anything else I had seen, to what lay at the core of the South's slave system—the chattel principle, human beings as property, as commodities, as merchandise. My God, I asked myself as I looked at the Betts & Gregory price list, how had we come to this?

So I decided to go into the belly of the beast to try to find out. I decided to read the surviving correspondence and study the account books and papers of Richmond's slave traders. If I could understand the traders and their agents and their customers, the parties who participated in the buying and selling of black men, women, and children on a daily basis, month after month, year after year, then maybe I could get my mind around some sort of answer to the question that has perplexed and troubled me for so long, the question I have been trying to answer, as I now realize, for as long as I have been studying history. Why did we not see the evil that was so clearly before us?

The shield in the upper left-hand corner of the circular suggested qualities that Betts & Gregory undoubtedly wanted the public to associate with their firm: security, stability, strength, permanence. "Betts & Gregory, AUCTIONEERS, Franklin Street, RICHMOND, VA." read the lettering inside the shield. No hastily handwritten list of prices current this, as other less prominent firms were wont to send out. No fly-by-night outfit here. The partners had gone to the trouble and expense of having a stack (in all probability many stacks) of these forms printed up so that, courtesy of their auction house, buyers and sellers could get clear, up-to-date information on the state of Richmond's "Negro Market."

Any vibrant market relies on a steady flow of accurate information, and the buying and selling of slaves in late antebellum
Richmond was a very vibrant market indeed. Agents out in the
field looking to make purchases for local firms needed these figures
badly and on a daily basis. Other traders and auctioneers in the
city undoubtedly studied these lists with great care. The hordes
of buyers up from the Deep South—slave dealers, planters, con-
tractors, industrialists, those seeking to acquire a young, attractive
female through the "fancy trade"—all had to have a sense of the
market to guide their purchases or their bidding on the auction
floor. Frequent articles on the trade in the Richmond press suggest
that the average man in the street followed the market closely as
well. Booms have a way of stirring hopes and dreams even among
those without the means to jump in.

The grading categories—"Extra," "No. 1," "Second rate or Ordinary" ("do." was the abbreviation for "ditto")—listed on Betts &
Gregory's circular reflected a variety of attributes. Age and overall
appearance were basic. A young man from his late teens to approximately twenty-six and a woman slightly younger, say seventeen to
her early twenties, would normally fall into the "No. 1" category.
For men, these ages marked their full physical development and
often their peak strength; for women, these ages placed them at
or near the peak of their childbearing years.

Obvious defects would knock a slave, even in these prime age
groups, into the "Second rate or Ordinary" classification—things
like the mark of a whip, faulty "action" (revealed by how well or
poorly a slave walked or ran around the auction floor), evidence
of past disease, unexplained scars or lumps on the body, a wheeze,
a cough, flawed teeth, even a bad attitude displayed on the block.
And, as will be discussed more fully later, there was a grade even
lower than "Second rate or Ordinary"; these were called "scrub"
Negroes, but Betts & Gregory did not list this category on their
circular—no need to suggest that the firm even trafficked in such

human merchandise, even though in fact they did, and there were buyers who specialized in this trade.

Elevation into the "Extra" classification could come about for a variety of reasons. Exceptional height or musculature, physical attractiveness, and special skills (blacksmithing or carpentry for men, for example, cooking or sewing for women) were among the attributes that could make a slave "Extra" in the eyes of the trade. Skin color could as well. "Black" was prized for field workers, male or female, lighter skin tones ("yellow" or "brown" or "mulatto") for house servants.

The fact that children were sold by height may be the most appalling feature of this appalling document. The listing began at "4 feet high" for both "Boys" and "Girls" and moved up by three-inch increments to "5 feet high" (manifests of slave ships engaged in the coastal trade, Richmond to New Orleans, for example, indicate that boys and girls as young as seven or eight years old often met the beginning height of four feet).[2] These Betts & Gregory listings for children also suggest that boys and girls of this age and size could be purchased separately from their parents, as indeed they were.

Equally appalling is the first handwritten line of the more detailed market report added by Betts & Gregory's clerk in the blank space under the printed price column: "Good young woman & first child $1300 to $1450." This mother and child "combination package" (my wording) was a staple of the Richmond slave trade. Proven childbearing ability commanded a premium, a clear reflection of the buyer's expectation of potential future increase in the owner's human capital if such a purchase were made. Another frequently used term to describe this category of female slave was "breeding woman." Such women were considered an ideal wedding present among more affluent white southerners. What could be more appropriate for a young couple just starting out? Indeed, it was not uncommon in these same circles for a white newborn infant to receive as a gift an older slave child of the same gender. A servant for life, as it were, who could be purchased by height on Betts & Gregory's auction floor.

On the firm's printed form, space was left after each category for a daily high and low price to be filled in. These figures would give a ready summary of where the market stood on any given day. As noted above, the clerk would then add supplementary information (like the price of a "Good young woman & first child") and whatever general guidance or commentary the principals of the firm wished to pass along.

The circular dated August 2, 1860, indicated a robust slave market in Virginia's capital city. Extraordinarily high prices were being paid for the most desirable classes of men, women, and children, a reflection of the strong demand for slaves in the booming agricultural areas of the Deep South:

Extra Men, $1,550 to $1,625.

No. 1 Men, $1,450 to $1,550.

Extra Girls, $1,375 to $1,450.

No. 1 Girls, $1,300 to $1,350.

Boys and Girls five feet in height, $1,100 to $1,250.

Even the youngest and smallest children listed in the circular, four feet high, were bringing $500 to $600 dollars each.

This market strength in 1860 continued a trend set in the previous decade as the worldwide demand for cotton soared to new heights. The *Richmond Enquirer,* the city's leading newspaper with a readership scattered across much of the South, carried a story on July 29, 1859, entitled "Our Slave Market." The article was brimming with optimism. "The price of cotton, as is well known, pretty much regulates the price of slaves in the South, and a bale of cotton and a 'likely nigger' are about well-balanced in the scale of pecuniary appreciation," the writer noted.

"In looking around at the slave sales in Richmond . . . we find that active negroes, likely families, as well as boys and girls, command high prices, and there are several gentlemen in the market who are purchasing for their own plantations in the South."

The report continued with a list of "the average prices brought by slaves in Richmond," figures that were offered, the writer added, "for the benefit of our country and Southern readers":

No. 1 men, 20 to 26 years old, $1,450 to $1,500.

Best plough boys, 17 to 20 years old, $1,350 to $1,425.

Boys from 15 to 17 years old, $1,250 to $1,375.

Boys from 12 to 15 years old, $1,100 to $1,200.

Best grown girls, 17 to 20 years old, from $1,275 to $1,325.

Girls from 15 to 17 years old, $1,150 to $1,250.

Girls from 12 to 15 years old, $1,000 to $1,100.

"Of course the quotations only represent the rates offered for the best class of slaves," the writer concluded. "The inferior grades are numerous and command prices in accordance with the qual ity."

Several things are noteworthy about this newspaper article. The cold, calculating, and sometimes celebratory tone speaks for itself. A boom was underway. The writer's assumption that the paper's "country and Southern readers" would be interested in this information also suggests a South-wide fascination with the Richmond market. Readers across the region could calculate their own wealth if they owned slaves or gauge what it would take to acquire one if they did not. And, most revealingly, the fact that the cotton price "pretty much regulates the price of slaves in the South," as the writer put it, speaks to the absolutely critical importance of the interstate slave trade as an engine of antebellum southern prosperity. That engine powered the boom in the cotton- (and sugar-) growing areas of the Deep South and, to a considerable degree, boosted the prosperity of the commonwealth of Virginia as well.

My ancestor Thomas Roderick Dew had freely acknowledged in 1832 that "Virginia is in fact a *negro* raising state for other states," and he cited this as one of the compelling reasons Virginians should not abandon the institution in the wake of Nat Turner's bloody 1831 uprising. His frank admission that his beloved state had a cash crop consisting of human beings—"she produces enough for her own supply and six thousand for sale," he went on to say—did not seem to embarrass him in the slightest. Indeed, he seems to have reveled in this supposed good fortune.

There were some notable omissions in the *Enquirer*'s 1859 market report, however. No mention was made of a key sales category: "Good young woman & first child." Nor does the practice, common among Richmond auction houses, of listing children for sale by height appear in the report. Indeed the lowest age mentioned for "Boys" and "Girls" is twelve. The "4 feet high" category that regularly appeared on auction firms' prices current broadsides dropped that age limit, as pointed out earlier, to seven or eight. Perhaps these items were omitted because the writer or the editor considered them inappropriate for a newspaper read widely by both men and women across the South (and frequently quoted by newspapers in the North as well).

These dollar figures from the late antebellum era may not mean much to modern readers, but they were, even by the standards of that day, astonishing. We do have a means of translating them into values for our own time, however. The very useful website MeasuringWorth.com, sponsored by the University of Illinois at Chicago, indicates that one 1860 dollar should be multiplied by a factor of approximately 29 to get that earlier dollar into contemporary purchasing power.[3]

Thus the August 2, 1860, Betts & Gregory figures would look something like this today:

Extra Men priced at $1,550 to $1,625 in 1860 would be $44,950 to $47,125.

Extra Girls ranging from $1,375 to $1,450 would be $39,875 to $42,050.

No. 1 Men priced from $1,450 to $1,550 would be $42,050 to $44,950.

No. 1 Girls listed at $1,300 to $1,350 would be $37,700 to $39,150.

The tallest category of Boys and Girls, five feet in height, priced at $1,100 to $1,250 in 1860 would be $31,900 to $36,250.

The "Good young woman & first child" ranging from $1,300 to $1,450 would represent $37,700 to $42,050 in contemporary purchasing power.

Even the prices for the smallest children listed as a separate sales category, four feet high, $500 to $600, would translate into five-figure sums today: $14,500 to $17,340.

Betts & Gregory's August 2 price report ended on a cautionary note, however. There was an ominous and ever-darkening cloud on the horizon in the late summer of 1860. "The market is dull this week owing to the fact that there are but few Southern buyers in the market," the firm's clerk wrote. A more optimistic final sentence pertaining to those "Southern buyers" (apparently written the day before) stating "We do not look for this to continue" had been crossed out as the principals of the house updated their assessment and tried to gauge where the market was moving.

A profound uncertainty was hovering over the South as summer lengthened and the fall elections approached. In mid-May, the Republican National Convention meeting in Chicago had nominated as the party's presidential candidate Abraham Lincoln of Illinois, a man almost all white southerners believed to be an abolitionist. To compound this naked act of supposed aggression, the Republicans had chosen as Lincoln's running mate someone widely rumored in the South to be a black man. Under the heading "Pedigree of Hannibal Hamlin," the *Charleston Mercury* summed up this notion when it reported as fact the claim "that Hamlin had negro blood in his veins, and that one of his children had kinky hair." As further proof, the *Mercury* added that "Hannibal and Scipio are both favorite names on the plantation."[4]

To make matters worse, in the wake of Lincoln's and Hamlin's nominations, the Democratic Party committed political suicide. Meeting in Charleston, South Carolina, in early May, the Democrats had split into bitterly antagonistic North-South wings, each of which nominated its own presidential ticket the following month. With Democratic forces thus divided, Lincoln's election looked increasingly likely. By early August, when Betts & Gregory's circular went out, the slaveholding South was beginning to come to grips with the prospect that an abolitionist might well occupy the White House and that a Negro might be a heartbeat away from the presidency. Little wonder that the principals of the firm of Betts & Gregory advised that it was time to exercise some caution in business matters. If confidence, and those "Southern buyers," did not return, there was no way the prices reported in their August 2 circular could last.

Richmond, Virginia, and firms like Betts & Gregory, Auctioneers, stood at the apex of a vast domestic slave-trading empire. In the summer of 1860, major Richmond newspapers carried standing advertisements from the leading auction houses that ran every day, week after week, month after month:

"BY BETTS & GREGORY, AUCTS. TWENTY NEGROES.— This day, at 10 o'clock, we will sell 20 likely slaves. Betts & Gregory, Aucts., Franklin Street."

Dickinson, Hill & Co., Aucts., "Fifty Negroes."

Hector Davis, Auct., "50 Negroes."

Pulliam & Co., Auctioneers, "25 Negroes."

Davis, Dupree & Co., Aucts., "30 Negroes."

Browning, Moore & Co., "twenty likely Negroes."

Moore & Dawson, Aucts., "12 Negroes."[5]

To look at column after column like this is bone-chilling. These standing advertisements, like the Betts & Gregory broadside that hit me with such force, are indicative of a world of unspeakable human degradation and exploitation. And what makes this trafficking in human beings even more horrific is that it was such a normal feature of the world in which white southerners lived, so commonplace, so accepted. Again, how could this be so? Perhaps the slave traders' correspondence would help me, would help all of us, answer this profoundly depressing but all-important question.

5

The Correspondence

PART I

I send over some good stock. . . .

It is hard to know where to start this discussion of the Richmond slave traders and their clients. Reading this correspondence now is like opening the door to a very dark room. We know something frightful and horrific lurks inside, and yet we know we must enter and search for the light. Not only to illuminate what is there but to make sure that those of us who are of and from the South, all of us, do not forget it or, even worse, try to pretend that it did not exist.

I have thought long and hard about how to present this material. Much of it is fragmentary, and like almost all business correspondence, it focuses largely on the ordinary, the everyday, the routine that constituted the warp and woof of the slave trade. But in some ways, that is what gives this material its enormous power: it was all, as was pointed out earlier, so mundane. The matter-of-fact way in which traders and their agents and their customers spoke about the buying and selling of men, women, and children, of all ages, of all "grades" of "quality," is as revealing as anything I have encountered in all the years I have been trying to understand the place where I was born and raised.

I decided to break the correspondence down into three broad

categories: letters written by traders to other slave traders; letters written between the traders' field agents—either independent or in-house buyers—and the Richmond dealers; and letters exchanged by the traders and their customers, both those seeking to buy and those looking to sell slaves.

By far the largest number of letters I found fall into the trader-to-trader category. It is hard to know if this is an accident of history or if the bulk of the slave traders' correspondence was indeed between men who followed the same dismal occupation. As far as I can tell, nothing approaching a full record of the activities of any Richmond slave trader has survived. And if two intrepid Yankee sisters had not set out to visit Richmond in 1865 shortly after Union troops occupied the city, we almost certainly would not have the record that we do.

Sarah and Lucy Chase, well educated and raised in a wealthy Quaker family in Worcester, Massachusetts, had gone to Virginia in 1862 to work among the "contrabands," the name given by Union general Benjamin F. Butler in May of that year to slaves who had escaped into Federally controlled territory. As educators and missionaries, the Chase sisters carried out their humanitarian work with extraordinary zeal, and they were in a position to enter Richmond shortly after the city fell in April 1865.[1]

One of the first things the two sisters did was visit the abandoned offices of several of the city's leading slave traders. They swept up batches of correspondence and a number of bound volumes and carried this material home with them when they returned to Massachusetts. Eventually, this documentation found its way to the American Antiquarian Society in Worcester and the Library of Congress. Without the dedication and enterprise of Sarah and Lucy Chase and their determination to preserve at least some of the records of Richmond's slave dealers, historians attempting to get inside the minds of these men and their clients would have very little with which to work.[2]

The correspondence between the traders themselves seemed to me to be the best place to begin. How did these men—they were all men—view the business? What words did they use to describe the ongoing practice of their profession? What seemed to motivate them? What did they think about the men, women, and children they bought and sold? And, above all, I wanted to know if they ever gave voice to the human dimension of what they were doing.

As mentioned above, most of the extant material is fragmentary, usually only one or two letters from a single correspondent. There are, however, two series of letters that are an exception to this rule. Both date primarily from the 1840s. Both involve R. H. Dickinson & Brother, the leading slave-trading firm in Richmond. Both consist of letters sent from dealers in two major cities just to the north of Virginia's capital city, Washington, DC, and Baltimore, Maryland. Both tell a powerful and highly disturbing story.

Thomas Williams was one of Washington's major slave traders, and it is clear from the opening letter to Richard H. Dickinson that the commerce between these two men was a brisk one. "I draw on you today for fifteen hundred dollars, which you will please honor," Williams wrote on May 26, 1847. "I will send over some negroes very soon," he went on to say, but he warned, "Good negroes are scarce and hard to buy." Williams then asked a question that suggests one of the most hellish facts about the antebellum slave trade: "How are families selling, a woman & child, & a woman and 3 to 5 children"?[3] Conspicuous by its absence is any specific mention of "fathers" in this query.

Williams continued to ship slaves to Dickinson on a regular basis, and the two men seem to have corresponded almost daily in the summer of 1847.

On June 3, Williams wrote, "I paid $586 for a 16 year old girl a day or two ago, and $750 for a 20 or 21 year old man—Prices getting very high over this way."[4]

On June 6: "I send over some good negroes. . . . I checked on Farmers Bank of Va yesterday for $2,500."

On June 8: "I send you some good negroes. . . . I expect to send over some more stock in 4 or 5 days."

On June 9: "I have six agents out in the country buying, and you may look for negroes from me pretty often."

And then, on June 14, 1847, Thomas Williams told Richard Dickinson something remarkable. The letter did not start out that way. "I send over some negroes which I wish you to do the best you can with," he said, the usual opening line of his correspondence with the Richmond trader. But then Williams wrote this: "If I don't continue to buy and send over, other Traders will buy & send them over, and they will go into the market at any rate."

I was dumbstruck when I read this line. I had never seen anything like this in any of the traders' correspondence I had read up to this point, and I was near the end of my research at this juncture. Did this sentence, at long last, reveal a pang of conscience, a note of remorse, an expression of regret, from someone who had sold, and was selling, human beings as if they were livestock?

Unfortunately, I cannot answer this question. This single sentence was, and remains, the only hint of doubt I found expressed in the many hundreds of letters I read written by traders and their clients. If Thomas Williams had any moral uncertainty about his chosen profession, one would expect to see evidence of it elsewhere in his extensive correspondence with Dickinson. But no such expression exists in the additional material that has survived. Indeed, what we see expressed in his subsequent letters is more of the same callous disregard for the fate of the men, women, and children caught up in this dreadful commerce. If anything, the callousness only gets worse.

Four days later, on June 18, Williams penned a long letter to Dickinson that indicated he was ratcheting up his involvement in the trade. He enclosed a $5,000 draft on a Baltimore bank redeemable in thirty days, "which amount I would be pleased to have laid out in good No. 1 men." Dickinson was to "keep possession of the men until I send you other negroes, to sell to meet it, Boys & girls, &c." Williams repeated that he had "six agents in the country buying at this time" and would have no trouble dispatching "some more negroes the first of next week."

The Washington dealer was clearly assembling what the trade referred to as a "shipping parcel" of slaves for transportation to the Deep South. Putting together such "parcels" invariably wreaked enormous destruction on families. But the agricultural season was in full swing in the cotton and sugar fields to the south, and Williams undoubtedly anticipated a ready sale there and a sizable profit on his $5,000 investment.

Four days later, on June 22, Williams gave Dickinson an added prod about what he wanted for that "shipping parcel": "I want good black sound strong negro men, fair men, likely men & good men are the sort to buy." And, as he had promised earlier, the Washington dealer was forwarding a steady stream of women, boys, and girls to Richmond to cover his sizable bank draft. "I send over some negroes, you will please do the best you can with them," he wrote. "The woman with the yellow girl & boy is well qualified and ought to sell well—The little black boy has a large navel, do the best you can with him—I will send you over two or 3 women with one child each in a couple of days—I have all my agents in the country buying." (The presence of two "yellow" children in this shipment suggests the strong possibility of a white father, but Williams did not go into detail on this subject.)

As was the case with this letter, the routine human tragedy of the slave trade was often deepened by the inclusion of a specific set of circumstances. On June 28, 1847, Williams wrote from Washington that he had paid $800 for a woman and her children with the understanding that they were to be sent "out of the city." Subsequently, the seller's wife insisted that they be returned to

Washington, but Williams would have none of it. He was incredulous that the slaves' former mistress wanted "to have them brought here & *set free,* and to live as a *wife* to a *Mexican,* who is the father of her two youngest children." Williams added that the woman "is qualified certain," a "first rate washer & Ironer & cook," and "a good padling will make her bring a good price, which I want for them."

Williams concluded this June 28 letter by outlining in detail his buying and selling plans for the rest of the summer. "Write fully on the receipt of this how you think your market will range from the 1st to the 15th July—If your market will justify it, I will send you over some 40 to 60 and perhaps 75 negroes, between now and the 15th July," Williams informed Dickinson. The Washington trader indicated he was willing to risk a high-volume/low-profit strategy if his Richmond counterpart thought the market would accommodate such an approach. "I am determined to buy 150 from now to the 1st Sept.," he added. "If you will keep me well advised of your market, I will send over every negro I can buy & make $10. to $15. on."

Apparently the Richmond market sustained just such a strategy and then some. Williams continued to forward an ever-swelling stream of "good stock" to Virginia's capital city, "good negroes" all, he insisted, who should command top dollar. Among the slaves he dispatched on June 30, 1847, were "a strictly No. 1 woman 19 Sarah & child," for whom Williams expected to get $625 to $650, and "a No. 1 brown skin girl 18, Elizabeth, which I think will bring $600." Williams also notified Dickinson that he was sending "a girl 17 to 18, in the family way, cost $570," and he wanted the Richmond trader "to do the best you can for me with her." (Clearly, expectant mothers posed a higher risk than the ubiquitous "woman & first child" category and thus sold for a lower price.) "I have my agents out buying and prices are about as high here as there," he concluded. "I am paying $575 for No. 1 women

17 to 21. & $750 for No. 1. men—and they are scarce at that price."

The final extant communication from Williams to Dickinson came the following summer. "I send over some good stock, which I think will sell well," he wrote on August 19, 1848. "Please have them fixed up right, and sell them privately [or at] public Auction, as in your judgement they will do best." (The "fixed up right" process included, of course, new clothing and anything else that might enhance their appearance, and their value. Traders were known to use black shoe polish to mask gray hair, for example, and to employ a variety of other tricks to mask potential blemishes.) "Let me know by Telegraph what you think of the boys & girls, and how they will sell," the Washington trader concluded.

The record revealed in these letters is both crystal clear and, in one extraordinary moment, maddeningly opaque. The clarity is obvious. The formidable sums of money involved, the obsessive concern with the fluctuating state of the market, the almost total immersion in the day-to-day buying and selling of human beings, these things are central to everything Thomas Williams and Richard Dickinson did and communicated about. Yet there was that one statement, that singular expression of doubt or conscience or whatever it was, when Williams penned that comment on June 14, 1847—"If I don't continue to buy and send over, other Traders will buy & send them over, and they will go into the market at any rate." What are we to make of this?

In the end, I was forced to conclude, very little. The totality of Williams's and Dickinson's correspondence reveals an almost unfathomable level of heartlessness and a total disregard for the humanity of their highly valuable "merchandise." Thomas Williams and Richard Dickinson had commodified the black men, women, and children who passed through their hands. That commodification, above all, constituted the core of their activity and defined who *they* were as human beings. If a hint of doubt crept into Williams's consciousness, he seems to have swiftly closed it off into a hermetically sealed compartment of his mind. There was too much to do. There was too much money to be made. Time was short. The market was unpredictable. His six agents were out in the country buying. Richmond needed "stock." The Deep South needed "good black sound strong negro men, fair men, likely men & good men." Back to business.

A second set of letters addressed to R. H. Dickinson & Brother came from members of a major Baltimore slave-trading family, the Campbells. The firm of B. M. & W. L. Campbell was one of the largest in the city, and the two principals as well as other members of the family seem to have carried on a lengthy business correspondence with Richard Dickinson in the late 1840s and into 1850.[5] These letters, although not as numerous as those from Thomas Williams, tell a similar tale of man's inhumanity to man in the antebellum South.

The constant concern traders felt over runaways and disobedient slaves in general emerges clearly in three Campbell letters dating from 1847 and 1848. "I write merely to say tell the purchaser of that stout man George that he will be consulting his own interest to keep him under such guard as will insure him against the chance of an escape, otherwise he will run away sure as hell," Walter L. Campbell wrote Dickinson on June 20, 1847. Campbell described the man as "an idle vagabond unaccustomed to any sort of restraint & always has his own way—quite a pretty article to be taken care of in my opinion." On a supposedly brighter note, Campbell reported, "We are buying up a lot of negroes & after this week if there comes a spur in your market I will see you again." He had acquired "a No. 1 cook in every respect 24 years old can be warranted 1st rate—will she sell well," he asked. Campbell added, almost as an afterthought, that "she has an infant child almost white."[6] It does not take much imagination to come to the conclusion that this "No. 1 cook" was offered up for sale because a white man, in all probability her master, had fathered her "infant child."

On August 5, 1848, John S. Campbell, a younger member of the firm, wrote from Baltimore that he was sending one of their traveling agents to Richmond with another recalcitrant slave and his family. "Mr. Redgrave has in charge a man his wife and child all of which Walter has wrote to you fully about," he began. "What I would say is put him in a safe jail until sold and clear us of him get the money and deliver him." This man had "acted the damn rascal with us," Campbell noted, but—no surprise here—he still expected "a good price" for him. He also wanted "the beggar to wear Iron." What made matters worse in the eyes of the Campbell family was that this man had been a supposedly pampered slave before his unspecified act of disobedience. "He is a negro that my father raised and is competent to be valuable but is a damn cross grain rascal," he added. The man's wife was "a fine servant and well qualified," but she and their child were to go on the block as well. Indeed, Campbell wanted every Negro the firm had sent to Richmond sold "when it can be done to advantage," and he instructed Dickinson to "paddle all the crazy ones until their senses are right."[7]

Ten days later, on August 15, 1848, Carter L. Campbell, another young member of the Campbell clan, wrote Dickinson that he was sending the Richmond trader yet another discipline problem, a man named Felix, who was to be "*put . . . into Lumpkins jail* until $600 can be had for him—be *sure to put him into jail*—allow me to urge that point." Felix's wife, who had also been dispatched to Richmond, Campbell intended to take back to Baltimore "unless 650 can be had for her." He described her as "sound—fashionable enough to be a dispeptic."[8] Felix, like the other slaves discussed by the Campbells, would almost certainly pay a staggering price— permanent separation from his wife—for whatever he had done to stir the Campbells' ire.

These three letters reflect one of the most stunning facts about white expectations regarding slave behavior in the antebellum

South: whites genuinely believed slaves should be grateful for their enslavement. Obedience, loyalty, willing and faithful service, even love, all this and more were due masters and mistresses, modest compensation for whites' shouldering the manifold duties and burdens of being slave owners. Slaves who violated these expectations did so at their peril, and these letters from the Campbells show just how dangerous such displays of "ingratitude" could be.[9]

The Campbell family continued dealing with Richard Dickinson's firm in 1849 and 1850, and their subsequent letters are equally revealing.

"I have some 25 on hand good stock and buy every day but not low," B. M. Campbell wrote on July 11, 1849. "People wont sell at reduced prices."[10]

In early 1850, Campbell was forwarding regular consignments to Dickinson, and not surprisingly, the Baltimore dealer wanted up-to-date pricing information, a quick sale, and prompt payment for his human merchandise. "I send you a Lot of Negroes which I wish sold. I telegraph you to day to know how women with one child would go. No answer & only send you one of that kind," Campbell told the Richmond trader on February 4. "I will draw on you on the 7th for the sale of this lot on that day." He promised "to send another Lot of negroes First next week. I want you to write me particularly about women with one or 2 children." He concluded this letter with a postscript: "Most of the negroes offering with us are Family negroes. Great many women with one or 2 children."

Business remained brisk between the two firms as the month progressed. "I shall send you a Lot of Negroes on Sunday or Monday if they get in," Campbell wrote on February 8. "There is a great many negroes offering this week and I want to keep my buyers out. Telegraph me on Recpt if I can Draw for this Monday. I shall have a good lot to send down if they get in."

Campbell's buyers did not "get in," but that hardly slowed the

Baltimore trader down. The next day, Campbell told Dickinson he was sending him "a good Lot of Negroes which I have bought myself this week." He advised Dickinson that he was drawing on him for $6,000, which he would apply toward "a shipping Lot" he was building for the southern market. "I think from the present disposition [here] to sell that I can give you a Lot every week."

This series of letters ends a week later with Campbell dispatching "a Lot" to Richmond, accompanied, as usual, by one of the Campbells' traveling agents. "Some of my negroes that I intended sending are unwell from [a] Bad Cold & concluded to hold them until next week," he added. Once again, the Baltimore slave dealer demanded quick payment through a bank draft or from Dickinson's "Private means." And he concluded by saying "I think I shall be able to give you patronage enough from this [time] until spring to repay your favours."[11]

Even a cursory reading of this correspondence reveals several telling aspects of the Upper South slave trade: the well-established routine that stripped Maryland (and other border South areas) of thousands of marketable slaves (from owners who invariably demanded high prices) and the funneling of these men, women, and children through the Richmond market; the astonishing sums of money that traded hands; the instantaneous telegraphic communication of price data, market trends, and shipping information; and the use of the commercial banking system to move the very substantial funds involved in slave trading. Perhaps most illuminating of all is the language employed: "lot," "good stock," "shipping parcel" or "shipping lot," "woman with one child," "woman with one or 2 children," and the near-constant reference by traders to their "buyers out," sweeping up their human merchandise from the Maryland countryside.

As I went through these letters, the constant use of words like "stock" brought a powerful tendency into focus for me. It was clear that the slave dealers had adopted some of the nomenclature of the livestock industry into their business jargon. This was reinforced by two letters written in late 1859 by William H. Betts of the firm of Betts & Gregory, Auctioneers.[12] "Scrub negroes dull sale," he noted on December 28, 1859, a line he repeated three days later. "Scrub negroes dull sale. There came in this morning some Scrub buyers," he added, "and I hope we will be able to work them off after a while."[13]

"Scrub" is a livestock term describing an undersized, inferior specimen of a breed, often of mixed or unknown parentage—in other words, a "mongrel." To have the word "scrub" applied to human beings, just like the ubiquitous terms "stock" and "lot," is extremely telling about the traders' mindset, or so it seems to me. They were reducing the human beings they bought and sold to the status of animals; they were carrying their conception of white superiority and black inferiority about as far as one can carry these two pernicious beliefs.

There is another revealing aspect in the Williams and Campbell correspondence. The southern author Daniel R. Hundley insisted in *Social Relations in Our Southern States,* his fascinating 1860 treatise on southern society, that "nearly nine tenths" of the human commerce of the antebellum trade consisted of "refractory," "brutal," "vicious," or "otherwise diseased" slaves.[14] Discipline problems seem to have put several Campbell slaves on the road to Richmond, but the letters suggest that the violation of white expectations was the principal reason behind these cases. "Refractory," as defined by masters, may apply in these instances, but the dealers' comments make it clear that the vast majority of border-area slaves were caught up in the interstate trade for one reason and one reason only, the greed of both owners and traders, all of whom expected to enrich themselves at the appalling expense of other human beings.

And the fact that prominent Richmond slave traders were elected to important posts in the city's government suggests that there was little or no genuine opprobrium attached to their profession. As the historian Gregg Kimball tells us in his superb study of antebellum Richmond, several major traders served on the city council in the 1850s, men like Bacon Tait, the owner of a slave jail in downtown Richmond, and Nathaniel Boush Hill. We have encountered N. B. Hill before; he was a partner with Richard H. Dickinson in the firm of Dickinson, Hill & Co., the premier slave-trading firm in Virginia's capital city. Hill held a seat on the council from 1852 to 1854 and then served there again from 1857 through the entirety of the Civil War—nine consecutive years.[15]

Reading the letters of these men today can only be described as a profoundly depressing exercise. They are obsessively concerned with the state of the market. They are dripping with greed. They are almost totally devoid of any trace of humanitarian concern for the people they are buying and selling. When a slave in their charge becomes ill, it is the possible pecuniary loss that worries them. Over and over again, I was struck by the incredible callousness their words convey. I realize these are my twenty-first century sensibilities clashing with theirs from the nineteenth century. But even so, an objective approach to these letters—the sort of objectivity I was taught as a historian to embrace—is impossible to sustain.

Take, for example, the following letter.

Tabb Carter, a slave trader from the Tidewater county of Gloucester, wrote R. H. Dickinson on August 1, 1848, that he was sending thirty-one Negroes to the Richmond firm, "for you to do your best with." Carter wanted Dickinson to handle the sales personally, and he instructed the Richmond trader to "divide the children or manage the matter as you think best." Carter also demanded "your *lowest commission*" and told Dickinson to "fix them up as well as you can before the sale." Carter assured Dickinson that the two white men who were to deliver the slaves were "both gentlemen," and he authorized one of them, who was his brother-in-law, "to sign my name to all Bills of Sale." Finally, Carter insisted that he be paid "in Hundred dollar bills if you can get them of the best Bank you have." The most telling phrase in this document is the obvious one: "divide the children . . . as you think best."[16]

Or this letter from R. V. Tiffey, a dealer writing from King George Court House, Virginia, on February 7, 1847, to R. H. Dickinson & Brother, concerning the sale of a woman named Susan. "I saw Susan's master the day after I recd your note, & he requested me to say to you that it is his wish that you would sell Susan the first opportunity, whatever you can Get for her, as she is making so many complaints and as she says she is not sound." Tiffey was convinced that "it is all pretentious & false representations she is making with the hope of returning to King Geo to live with her husband which she will never do."

Or this letter, also dated February 7, 1847, from Robert Sanders, a Lynchburg trader, to R. H. Dickinson & Brother, informing the Richmond firm that, "if the market will do," he was sending down "a boy 12 or 13 likely[,] a black girl 15 years old likely but not large [and] a Yellow Girl about 11 years old tolerable good looking."

Or this communication from one B. P. Crabb of Westmoreland County to R. H. Dickinson & Brother, sent on February 23, 1847. Crabb was hoping to find a "bargan" and had been looking at "one or too boys" and thought he was near buying "one of them." He concluded this letter by asking the Richmond traders "whether you have sold Peggy & her too children, & if you have sold my little girl or the woman."

The system even corrupted some black southerners who became facilitators for the enslavement of other black southerners. A slave owner named James Mitchell wrote Richard Dickinson a remarkable letter on August 3, 1848, which was to be hand-delivered "by George Robinson a free man[,] the same man that was with me in Richmond and assisted me in trying to catch my runaway."

If George Robinson was successful in tracking down the present runaway, a man named Henry, the owner wanted Dickinson to sell Henry at a "good price" and give Robinson "$25 as this is the amt that I agree to pay him for catching this man Henry."

These letters, and many more like them, reflect what I have come to see as the twin hallmarks of Richmond's slave trade: pure, unalloyed avarice and a stunning disregard for the humanity of the thousands of men, women, and children thrust into this commerce. The corruption and depravity spread across the South by this trade was wide and deep. The contact might be direct, as in the case of the traders and owners and their human subjects, or it might be indirect, as in the case of southern society as a whole. But very few, if any, southerners of this era, black or white, were free from its contamination.

Antebellum white southerners considered slaves inferior human "stock." Slavery in that era, segregation in mine, were both cut from the same cloth. The overarching, unquestioned assumption of white superiority and innate black inferiority made all the difference in the world, for us in the twentieth century just as it did for my ancestors back in the nineteenth. There was more that bound us together than I could possibly have imagined.

6

The Correspondence

PART II

*... a very superior young woman such as you might
not find in riding a month.*

In July 1860, the slave trade continued to be a going concern in the commonwealth of Virginia. The political turmoil of the summer may have temporarily deranged the market, but the price circulars issued by Richmond traders were still very much in demand.

A man named C. B. Ackiss, a potential buyer for the well-established Richmond slave-trading firm of Browning, Moore & Co., wrote on July 3 that he was willing to act as their purchasing agent in Princess Anne County. "You asked me to direct my country-men who have servants to sell to your house, and you will divide the coms. [commissions]," Ackiss wrote. "I accept the proposition, and want you to send me the *prices currant* every week, that I may be able to give any information asked for." In conclusion, he added, "There is to be several family of negroes sold in this coming fall & winter in our county for [estate] division &c."[1]

This commodification of human beings in my ancestors' culture is very difficult for us to fathom today. The Betts & Gregory market circular from August 1860 is the rock that I happened to turn over that revealed so powerfully the stark reality of this world to me, and it was this document that sent me to the archives in search of answers. What follows in this chapter are representative samples of what I found in the letters of three sets of writers who corresponded with Richmond slave traders: the buyers of slaves, the sellers of slaves, and the traders' agents who traveled the countryside seeking the men, women, and children who would keep their principals' showrooms and auction houses stocked with human merchandise.

In many ways, these documents speak for themselves. But as any decent historian will tell you, "letting the documents speak for themselves" is frequently a way for scholars to mask laziness: an attempt to show off what we have found and avoid the hard work of interpretation, analysis, and the presentation of a coherent picture. So I have tried to strike a balance: allow the reader to get the flavor of this correspondence and, at the same time, to offer my thoughts on at least some of what these individual pieces of evidence tell us. I suspect readers will come to their own conclusions about much of this material. I hope very much that they do. But I also see it as my responsibility to comment and analyze; I have read a great deal of this correspondence now, and I have thoughts and opinions based on this exposure. I hope I have managed to strike the proper balance, but in the end that is up to the individual reader to decide.

The pressing need for up-to-date market information was omnipresent among buyers and sellers of slaves in the Old South. The Betts & Gregory circular that triggered this investigation of Richmond's slave traders and their customers turned out to be a fortuitous place to begin. It soon became evident that there was something close to an obsession among the parties engaged in the trade with these price circulars and the information that could be gleaned from them. Nowhere was this fixation more obvious than in the papers of James Brady, a general merchant and frequent slave buyer operating out of the James River town of Scottsville, some seventy-five miles west of Richmond and fifteen miles south of Charlottesville.

James Brady was a classic middleman who worked as an independent buyer or, on occasion, as an agent for one of the major Richmond traders. He would head out regularly on horseback and crisscross a number of central Virginia counties in search of slaves, usually buying on his own account and then reselling his human merchandise in Richmond as quickly as possible.

Since Brady normally made his initial purchases with his own funds, it was vitally important that he know, promptly and in detail, the state of the Richmond market. He relied on his business associates there to forward him a steady stream of reports on what was selling well, what was selling poorly, and what prices the various categories of slaves were bringing. Unlike the Betts & Gregory circular of August 2, 1860, the reports Brady received were entirely written out by hand, but in every other respect they are as chilling as the prices current document that lies at the heart of this book. And the picture that emerges from these letters is a remarkable one, even in the context of so much that is so profoundly depressing about the historical record of Richmond's antebellum slave trade.

Sidnum Grady, a long-time Richmond trader, did considerable business with James Brady and was a major source for his market data. Grady's letter of June 23, 1846, to the Scottsville buyer covered the Richmond market in what can only be described as extraordinary detail. "No.1 little girls 4 feet 5 to 7 inches high $275 to $300 very superior ones $325 to $350 and upwards according to make, countenance, intelligence &c.," Grady's letter begins (these three very revealing descriptive qualities appear more than once in this and subsequent letters). "All ungrown females in the same ratio—Likely and well made boys 4 feet 9 and 10 inches $375 to $450." Grady pointed out that this price range for "boys of the same height" again reflected the quality of the merchandise, specifically the "difference in countenance, make, intelligence &c."

Boys "5 feet 2 or 3 inches high $475 to $500. All boys the sizes whereof are not here specified will sell in like proportion to those named," he continued.

Only at this point in his letter did Grady turn to older slaves. "Likely woman with either few or many children will sell as readily as any and in price fully that proportion to the foregoing description that they usually do," he wrote (as usual, no mention of fathers here). "Really No. 1 Young fellows $550 to $600—Extra ones might go $625—Same class Young women $425 to 450. Very superior ones would perhaps reach $475," the Richmond dealer concluded the body of this letter.

But Sidnum Grady was not quite finished. He added a postscript that reflected a booming market and revealed an important element of his pricing strategy. "An Extra No.1 girl field hand tall and stout might go $500," he wrote. "So brisk is the demand and so great the scarcity of the kind of negroes I quote that I think each class quoted might go a few dollars over my quotations. Yet I will not change them because I had rather be under than over the mark." Grady was convinced that "this is the way to give information to persons for whom one sells and not induce them to pay too high." But whatever he did, Brady should get his purchases to Richmond as quickly as possible. "If you have got negroes [you] had better bring them for never since 1837 did I in the month of June see all sorts and kinds of negroes so scarce as now."[2]

Later that same summer, prices were rising so rapidly that Sidnum Grady started to worry. "No.1 little girls 4 feet 5 to 7 inches high" were going for $425 to $475, depending, of course, on "countenance, make, intelligence &c.," he wrote on August 22, 1846. Other categories of men, women, and children had risen proportionally. Grady then added a postscript that tells us a great deal about how James Brady went about his business. "Although a very superior young woman such as you might not find in riding a month sold the other day for $580 and an extra 6 foot young fellow at $750," Grady believed "that these prices will not long be sustained and that my quotations are as high as they should be for safety." Far better to err on the side of caution, he was saying. Markets can change in the blink of an eye; only the risk is constant.

Other market circulars that Brady received during the next few years followed the same general format, but revealing variations sometimes crept in. "Negroes are at a stand," wrote the Richmond firm of Hodges, Ray & Pulliam in March 1847. The coming of spring would soon lift prices, however, and "Breeding women & children will [be] selling better." But "No.2 Negroes" were "bad stock for the market" unless they were bargain priced. "Verry likely plough boys are selling best," they reported, but "boys too small to plough will not sell in proportion."[3] Clearly, one had to know the intricacies of the grading system and have up-to-date market information in order to prosper in this business.

Despite Brady's best efforts, he could not always time the market. Hodges, Ray & Pulliam advised Brady in May 1847 that he should return to Richmond with a lot of slaves he had previously been unable to sell. "Boys are selling as well as girls or a little better," wrote the firm's clerk. "I believe you can make a profit on the boys you had here some time ago if you could drop in to an auct House and sell them to the highest bidder." To underscore this point, the clerk noted that "Sales this morning" included a boy three feet ten inches tall at a good price.[4]

Letters from prominent Richmond auction houses with which Brady regularly did business in the 1850s give us additional insight into the language of the trade. "Good shipping negroes" was a term Pulliam & Slade employed, an obvious reference to those slaves who would command a premium price in the Deep South.[5] "Plough boys say 6 feet up" were selling well in the fall of 1854, Pulliam & Davis informed Brady, as were "No.1 Extra girls 16 to 18 with no defects Heavy set &c."[6] Later that same autumn, this Richmond firm reported that "good shipping men" were once again in demand, and "No.1 Black" men weighing 160 to 180 pounds were bringing as much as $1,200.[7] A circular from Dickinson, Hill & Co. in the spring of 1855 priced children by age instead of height and began at ten years old. A postscript advised Brady that "Extra No.1 Girls & Boys will command $50 above the prices quoted."[8]

We know Brady put this market information to malevolent use, and we know the devastation it caused. A Charlottesville slave woman named Maria Perkins informed her husband, Richard, on October 8, 1852, that one of their children had already been sold and that she and their other child might soon be as well—Richard and Maria Perkins were owned by different masters. "Dear Husband," she wrote, "I write you a letter to let you know my distress my master has sold albert to a trader on Monday court day and myself and other child is for sale also." Maria was clearly desperate, and she pleaded with Richard to do everything in his power to persuade his master or another slave owner in Richard's neighborhood to buy her and their remaining child. "I don't want a trader to get me," she continued; "a man buy the name of brady bought albert and is gone I don't know where he [Brady] lives in Scottesville." She ended the body of her letter with a lamentation: "I am quite heartsick." Her closing was a promise: "I am and ever will be your kind wife Maria Perkins."[9]

Even this brief sampling of traders' correspondence and the language and consequences of the slave marketplace more than validates a comment made by Frederick Law Olmsted, the most astute of all the northern observers who traveled across the South in the 1850s. Olmsted took note of what he called a "proverbial expression" among southerners that "Negroes are the *consols* of the South." When southern men likened slaves to "consols," they were comparing the market in human beings with the fluctuating market for "consolidated annuities," the funded securities issued in that era by the British government. "Men speak in railroad cars of 'turning off' so many negroes every year, precisely as a Connecticut farmer speaks of 'turning off' so many head of neat stock to the drovers every spring," Olmsted reported.[10]

These human *"consols* of the South" were used over and over again to bail their owners out of debt. Consider the following note of smug satisfaction in this letter written by a Virginian named Edmund Pate, as he reported from New Orleans that he had managed to extricate himself from a difficult financial situation. "The object of my trip to this Country was . . . to raise money to discharge the judmt. of [the] Spotts[ylvania court]," he wrote. "I have succeeded beyond my expectations—I have sold nearly all the negroes except two families, amounting to about ten or twelve—I have no doubts, that I shall be able to dispose of them in the course of ten days, when I shall set out immediately for home," he bragged. "I am now provided with the means of settling that claim. I pledge myself my honor and everything that is sacred, that the money shall be paid."[11] He had salvaged his "honor" by transporting his slaves to Louisiana and selling them off exactly as Olmsted had described, like "so many head of neat stock."

A similar situation—indebtedness and a desperate slave owner—emerges in a joint letter written by a father and son, Edmund and Alex Fitzhugh, of Falmouth, Virginia, dated February 16, 1846, and addressed to R. H. Dickinson, Richmond's largest slave trader.

The son, Edmund, led off. "My father has requested me to drop you a line & beg that you will not think of selling Lucy, for less than $500 & Maria for $450—unless you can get the prices above mentioned, he much prefers having them returned." The younger Fitzhugh went on to say that his father "was very much surprised & rather vexed at Godfrey's selling for only $571 & regrets extremely that he sent him down, as he could have gotten $600 for him here very readily."

Note what has transpired here. The father, seeking to maximize his profit on the sale of Godfrey, has sent him into the Richmond slave trade only to end up with less money than he could have gotten locally, or so he believes.

The father, Alex Fitzhugh, was so "vexed" that he added, in a very shaky hand, a lengthy postscript to his son's letter. "I really felt much disappointed at the low price of Godfrey. I could have most readily obtained six hundred dollars for him here—and then only to get 571 is distressing," he complained to Dickinson. Alex Fitzhugh then revealed the source of his distress: he was "compelled to raise 2100 dolls." Not only had Godfrey's price been a disappointment, his son's expenses in taking him to Richmond "amounted to upwards of fifty dollars."

At this point in his letter, Alex Fitzhugh basically fell to his knees and begged. "*Do my old friend I beseech* try if in your power to get nine hundred fifty [for Lucy and Maria] if practicable they would have brought that here—but if that cannot be obtained, as they are in Richmond, take a a [*sic*] little less, as I have incurred already very heavy expense." The much-troubled elder Fitzhugh closed with one more plea: "Do my old friend the best you can."[12]

So in his quest for $2,100 to meet a pressing debt, Alex Fitzhugh had turned his back on a possible local sale, one presumably Godfrey, Lucy, and Maria would have much preferred, and thrust this man and these two women into the maw of the Richmond slave trade. And then, lo and behold, Godfrey had sold for less in Richmond than the Fitzhughs believed they could have obtained locally. No wonder the older Fitzhugh was vexed and distressed. And note the cause of his frustration; it had nothing to do with the fate of these three lives. It rested on his bitter disappointment at making a bad bet: that his slaves would sell for top dollar in Richmond, including enough to cover the expense of conveying them to the city and boarding them until sale.

The Fitzhugh clan apparently spread word of their vexation around Falmouth. A neighbor, one James M. Pelby, had also dispatched a slave girl to Richmond with young Fitzhugh but was now having second thoughts. "From what I have heard from Mr. Fitzhugh of the prices in Richmond for such girls as the one I sent down by him . . . I think I can do a great deal better than that in this neighbourhood where she is known," Pelby wrote Dickinson on February 23, 1846. He instructed the Richmond trader to send her back by rail with "a note to Port royal," but he added one final caveat: "if you can get five hundred for her you can let her go."[13] The fact that this "slave girl" was "known" "in this neighbourhood" came into his calculations for one reason and one reason only: the price she might command.

Even when a trace of concern over the fate of a slave creeps into a letter, that sentiment almost invariably disappears when dollar signs pop up. "I send down . . . a negro boy (Charles) whom I wish you to sell for me as soon as you can without making a sacrifice in doing so," a man named John G. Skelton of Powhatan County wrote R. H. Dickinson in February 1846. Skelton described Charles as "an intelligent sprightly boy" who was "raised as a dining room servant," and his owner evidenced some concern for Charles's fate. "If you can dispose of him in Richmond or in such a way that he will not leave the state, for what you may consider his value or near it, I would be glad," Skelton wrote. The decided limits of this owner's concern for Charles were reflected in his concluding statement on the matter: "I presume you have applications for servants of particular descriptions—but I had rather you should not make much delay in the sale." Skelton closed this letter by asking what he could expect to make from the sale of another slave, this one "a well formed negro woman with a likely child, the former about 23 or 24 & the latter 2 years old, both mulatto complexion."[14] In this instance, he expressed no concern about how this mother and child might be disposed of and where they might end up.

The dehumanization of this form of human property is a near constant in the traders' correspondence.

S. C. Pender of Tarboro, North Carolina, asked R. H. Dickinson on February 8, 1846, "whether you have sold the negroes Cato & Tempy left at Mr. Lumpkins' Jail and if not I wish you to sell them as soon as you can conveniently and if you have not sold inform me when you think you can sell and the price you think you can get." He closed with a near-ubiquitous question in the traders' correspondence, one that reflects the obsessive concern with the state of the market. What, Pender asked, is "the price of negro fellows and Girls no.1 and whether you think the prices improving or not."[15] One suspects strongly that if Pender received a positive response to this query, more of his human chattel would soon be on the road to Richmond.

A follow-up letter from Pender to Dickinson on February 27 instructed the Richmond dealer to sell "the negro man Cato...and the woman Tempy...as soon as possible." Their impatient master explained that "I don't want them upon expense no longer than can be helped." Traders' daily charges for room and board obviously added up and cut into the seller's profit. And, not surprisingly, Pender wanted to know "the state of the slave market" as well.[16]

Consider this agent's profoundly revealing definition of misfortune. "I lost the Boy Emerson that Henry Davis bought from Hall of Norfolk for me. He died last night [after] 48 hours sickness. *hard luck* as some would say," N. C. Trowbridge wrote R. H. Dickinson & Brother from Augusta, Georgia, on March 14, 1850. But Trowbridge went on immediately to say that he had had some better luck. "I exchanged your Boy Patrick today & got a No. One Boy 18 & fifty Dolls," a transaction he gleefully described as "a first rate trade—I made for you."[17] From misfortune to good fortune in no more time than it might take to turn over a card on a poker table. But there was even more good news. "I sold the Boy George that I swap[p]ed Patrick for, and got 850 payable first Jany [January] next," he wrote Richard Dickinson three weeks later. "The paper is No. One so you perceive Patrick will bring you 900

Dolls next Jany." He also reported that he found "Reuben better & not so many sick."[18] Fortune did indeed seem to be smiling on Trowbridge and his principal back in Richmond.

Or take the following letter written in 1857 to Richard Dickinson's new firm, Dickinson, Hill & Co., describing the fate of a slave girl caught up in the settlement of an estate. "I send over a negro girl Tina by name—belonging to the children of B. F. Dabney decd of whom I am guardian—to be sold," wrote W. B. Newton of Hanover County, Virginia. "The girl will be sold for no fault—the necessities of the family being such as to render the sale imperative."[19] As Frederick Law Olmsted had so perceptively noted, slaves were indeed "the *consols* of the South," ready to be turned into cash at a moment's notice.

Or witness the insane contradictions in this letter, written by one L. Wilkes of Liberty, Bedford County, Virginia, to Dickinson, Hill & Co., dated July 11, 1855: "If you have not sold Charles you had better have his life ensured for two or three months. I am determined to sell him but I do not want to sacrifice him, try and get him to talk right, probably you will have to have him whiped a few times before he will do [that]." So here is the plan: insure the life of my chattel and then lay on the lash, multiple times if necessary, to my very valuable piece of human property. Wilkes's final comment? "Let me hear what is the prospect of the market."[20]

Or note the appalling implications of this letter, penned by William F. Cocke Jr. of Brandy Station, Virginia, on October 15, 1860, and addressed to Dickinson, Hill & Co.: "What can you sell a large likely and well qualified woman 24 years of age for?" Why was she being sold? The answer came in these words: "How can I buy a few boys and girls from 8 to 15 years of age? I may want to buy 10 or 15 negroes."[21]

This manuscript litany of man's inhumanity to man can be extended almost indefinitely. The Richmond traders' correspondence is replete with countless additions to what has been cited here. I thought, however, an appropriate place to conclude this chapter would be with two letters that suggest the utter vulnerability that the chattel principle—human beings as property—inflicted on the African American men, women, and children caught up in the Old South's slave system.

One would like to think that someone who found themselves ensnared in these unimaginable circumstances might have one way out, a way that fell short of attempting to flee their bondage and thus put themselves at risk of near-certain sale or brutal punishment or both. Might there not be another way to afford oneself at least a chance at some stability, some possible protection against sale? Could one not work hard and diligently, appear deferential and humble, give evidence of loyalty, even affection, toward master and mistress, acquire valuable skills, and generally make oneself into that proverbial "good and faithful servant" that antebellum southern whites so extolled? Think again.

The first letter was written by J. Hobbs of Chesterfield Court House, Virginia, on February 17, 1846, to R. H. Dickinson & Brother. "I send up this morning…a negro girl named Lucy which I wish you to sell for the best possible price," Hobbs instructed. "She is about 17 years of age and a stronger healthier or more valuable girl I believe cannot be found." Her qualifications? "She is a very good seamstress, she can cut and make a dress very neatly and make shirts pants and in fact almost anything she chooses, and a better house servt you do not often find." So why is she marked for sale? "I sell her because I have no use for her, having enough girls without her, and wanting the money to lay out for a man." How should this talented seventeen-year-old girl be sold? "Please sell her publicly or privately as you think you can do best." How marketable is she? "If there is any girl that ought to bring a good price I think this one ought."[22]

To use a livestock reference that does not seem at all inappropriate here, J. Hobbs of Chesterfield Court House, Virginia, is "thinning his herd." And he has sent out of his human flock a very valuable "animal" named Lucy, someone who has trained herself to do important work, is highly skilled at what she does, can do multiple jobs (sewing, house servant), and is, in Hobbs's humble opinion, "stronger healthier" and "more valuable" than any seventeen-year-old girl he can possibly imagine. So what has this earned her? The Richmond slave trade. Hobbs needs a man, and if he is to "lay out" sufficient funds to acquire a first-rate male, he decides to sell a first-rate female. Lucy has made herself just that. Her reward is about as bitter a pill as one can imagine a young girl, or anyone else for that matter, being forced to swallow.

The second letter that illuminates the vulnerability of even the most "good and faithful servant" is a single document in the papers of James Brady, the Scottsville slave buyer discussed earlier, who rode across multiple counties in central Virginia looking for prize human merchandise.

Let me interject here that I have purposely tried to avoid the use of block quotations in the presentation of this correspondence because I know their frequent inclusion invites the reader to skim. The eye tends to move quickly from the beginning to the end of a block quote, whether we intend this or not. I hope this will not happen here, because I want to offer this letter for a single, close reading. I think it is the sort of document that those who have read this far in this study will have their own well-informed opinions about. I will have some things to say as well, of course, but the reader will certainly see multiple layers here, in all probability things I have missed.

This letter, written by John W. Abrams of Buckingham, Virginia (a rural area south of Charlottesville), is addressed to James Brady, Esq., and is dated July 20, 1852:

To the strong and constant appeals of my wife not to let Harriett go yet I am obliged to yeal[d]. Therefore I write you this simply to say that I have prosponed the selling of her for *a while*. My wife says that she thought I was joking when I spoke of selling her otherwise she never would have given her consent—I am however *determined* to sell her & that before very long and I say to you that you must hold yourself in readiness to buy her whenever I can procure the consent of my wife again to part with her.

Harriett is the best servant we own & when gone I never expect to get her place filled, but as I before said she is worth too much for us to keep and the balance of our negroes are in families which I hate to part.

When I let you know that my wife has given her consent you must come forthwith and get her . . . (that is if you conclude to give the price) for I want to avoid if possible a big *hurrah*.[23]

So what are we to make of this? It seems to me, once again, that the insane contradictions inherent in the trafficking of human beings are on full display here.

First, Harriett herself.

Abrams describes her as "the best servant we own." This alone suggests that Harriett has performed her work admirably, certainly in the eyes of his wife, and, indeed, she has done her work so well that Abrams says "I never expect to get her place filled" once Brady has carried her off.

It may be total speculation, but I think it may well be that Harriett has tried to make herself indispensable by working hard and working well. It is also entirely possible that she was yielding to what I suspect is a basic human instinct to try to do something to the best of one's ability, even though in this case she is enslaved and cannot reap anything like the full fruits of her own labor. But, without question, she has, for whatever reason, rendered "good and faithful service" to the Abrams household.

So what, in the end, has Harriett, this slave woman, managed to do? She has miraculously accomplished something close to impossible: she has simultaneously rendered herself completely ir-replaceable and totally expendable. As Abrams himself so bluntly explained, she had made herself "worth too much for us to keep." Some calamity might befall her—injury, disease, even death could occur at any time—and clearly Abrams did not want to miss out on the formidable amount of money Harriett would bring when she went into the slave trade. Indeed, we can imagine him lying awake nights worrying about these nightmarish scenarios and scheming of ways to persuade his wife to let her go.

Abrams goes on in the sentence quoted just above to offer a second reason Harriett must go: "the balance of our negroes are in families which I hate to part."

Admirable on this slave owner's part, we might be tempted to say, keeping families together, not separating husband from wife, parent from child. But on closer inspection, several other factors may be at work here. Slaves remaining behind after family members have been sold off could become angry or morose or turn into disciplinary problems, perhaps even become violent. Slave men, women, and children running away to try to rejoin loved ones was an everyday phenomenon in the Old South. So why, Abrams may have thought, run these risks? Besides, husbands and wives who already had children might well have more. Since every healthy birth was an addition to the master's wealth, why give that up? Harriett apparently was unmarried, but that was not why Abrams was "*determined* to sell her & that before very long." She was, to repeat, to be sold for one reason and one reason alone: "she is worth too much for us to keep."

So Abrams hatches an elaborate plot to effect Harriett's sale. His wife "thought I was joking when I spoke of selling her" and ap-parently went along with this "joke" at first. But then Mrs. Abrams sobered up, as it were. "Not on your life," we can imagine her say-ing. But her husband is undeterred and is certain he can prevail in the end. So, he tells Brady, "you must hold yourself in readiness to buy her whenever I can procure the consent of my wife again to part with her," and "you must come forthwith and get her."

There is, of course, one final matter to be resolved. Yes, Brady, when I send word come at a gallop, but only, repeat only, "if you conclude to give the price." In the end, it always comes down to the price.

We do not know Harriett's fate. This single letter is the only document we have concerning her. But if I had to speculate, I would have to guess that she was sold, first to James Brady and then from a Richmond slave jail or auction block or a trader's private showroom to a buyer, one who could afford an "Extra Girl," to quote the top female category in Betts & Gregory's 1860 market circular. Given the ever-rising prices slaves commanded in the 1850s and the near-universal prevalence of greed as the dominant force motivating white southerners to buy, sell, and trade human "stock" in the late antebellum years, optimism regarding Harriett's fate is very hard to come by. In this male-dominated culture, to expect the mistress, Abrams's wife, to remain steadfast in opposition to her husband under these circumstances is expecting a very great deal indeed.

There is no mystery about the fate of James Brady. As he lay on his deathbed early in 1857, the human vultures were already circling. A Scottsville business associate of his, J. W. Mason, fired off an urgent letter to Dickinson, Hill & Co. on February 28 of that year instructing the Richmond slave traders to impound immediately any funds due Brady. "There is, I understand, a negro woman Sally & child belonging to James Brady left in your possession," Mason wrote, and his understanding was "that an agent would be dispatched to day to get the proceeds" of this sale and also the money realized from an earlier sale for Brady of "some 8 or 10 negroes." The pending arrival of the agent prompted Mason to issue a stern warning: do not release any funds due Brady. There was an "insufficiency of property by a very large amount to pay his debts," and Brady's "extreme illness" was fast reaching a climax. "Mr. James Brady . . . cannot breathe more than 3 or four hours from this time 11' O clock A.M.," Mason informed the Richmond traders, "and as the creditors of the estate would hold you responsible for the money if paid to the wrong person after his death," the money definitely should not be turned over to the agent. Brady's "death," Mason assured Dickinson, Hill & Co., "will inefitably take place before this reaches you," and he was writing them "for your own benefit as well as that of myself." As it turned out, Brady's Scottsville business associate was "security for the purchase of the negro [Sally and her child] & will have most of it to pay even if the proceeds are legally applied."[24]

One searches in vain in J. W. Mason's letter for even a hint of sympathy for the soon to be late, and apparently unlamented, James Brady, Esq. Mason's sole concern is for the control of Brady's assets, a concern that precedes his actual demise by at least "3 or four hours." Given the untold misery James Brady brought to countless slave men, women, and children during the course of many years riding the central Virginia countryside looking for his next Harriett to carry off to Richmond, it is impossible even at this distance to muster any desire to say what Mason studiously avoided saying in his letter to Dickinson, Hill & Co.: "James Brady, may he rest in peace."

7

The Market

Sells Negroes both publicly and privately, and pledges his
best efforts to obtain the highest market prices.

Between 1790 and 1861, over one million slaves were transported
from the Atlantic coastal states to the interior regions of the Upper
and Lower South. The historian Ira Berlin refers to this forced mi-
gration as a "Second Middle Passage," a movement "dwarfing the
transatlantic slave trade that had carried Africans to the [North
American] mainland."[1] Some of these men, women, and children,
particularly in the early decades, went with their owners, who were
moving to inland areas where bonanza crops of cotton and sugar
could be grown. But after 1820, a clear majority of the slaves carried
south were shipped by professional slave traders. Michael Tadman,
who has done the most thorough study of this process, estimates
"a share of at least some 60–70 percent for the trade" in the four
decades leading up to the Civil War.[2] By 1860, the dimensions of
the traffic in slaves had reached staggering proportions. "The internal slave trade became the largest enterprise in the South outside
of the plantation itself, and probably the most advanced in its
employment of modern transportation, finance, and publicity,"
Berlin correctly notes.[3]

Two historians have recently offered detailed figures that support Berlin's generalizations. James L. Houston in 2003 estimated
that the value of slave property in the South in 1860 stood at $3 bil-

lion, an "unbelievable amount of wealth . . . compared with other sectors of the United States economy in 1860." Unbelievable indeed. That $3 billion figure "was almost 50 percent more than the $2.2 billion invested in railroads and manufacturing" in the entire country in 1860, Houston pointed out.[4] Another historian, Steven Deyle, writing in 2004, noted that the value of "slave property had surpassed the assessed value of real estate" in the South, which stood at just over $2.4 billion.[5] These incredible figures for the value of the South's slave population in 1860 were made possible by two critical and interrelated developments: the fact that slave prices more than tripled in New Orleans (the prime market in the Lower South) in the nineteenth century—a prime field hand who sold for $500 in 1800 would command $1,800 in 1860;[6] and the development of the domestic slave trade into exactly what Ira Berlin called it, "the largest enterprise in the South outside of the plantation itself," a gigantic engine of human trafficking, moving hundreds of thousands of men, women, and children from the Upper to the Lower South in the first six decades of the nineteenth century.

Historians like James Houston and Steven Deyle have done us a distinct service by pointing out the comparative value of the South's human property in 1860, but I think they may have been too cautious in setting the value of that property. Their $3 billion figure assumes an average price of $750 for the close to 4 million human beings who made up the slave population in the South in 1860. A quick averaging of the prices for men, women, boys, and girls listed on the Betts & Gregory August 2, 1860, market circular yields a figure of just over $1,000 per slave, and this was the price in Richmond, not New Orleans. I think that $1,000 figure, multiplied by the 1860 slave population of almost 4 million, gives us a more accurate total, one that is closer to what contemporary southerners were estimating on the eve of the Civil War: $4 billion.

Stephen Fowler Hale, a commissioner dispatched from Ala-

bama to Kentucky in December 1860 to persuade the Kentuck-
ians to leave the Union, cited multiple reasons for secession,
but he was careful to emphasize that "African slavery" in "the
Southern States . . . constitutes the most valuable species of their
property, worth, according to recent estimates, not less than
$4,000,000,000; forming, in fact, the basis upon which rests the
prosperity and wealth of most of these States."[7]

And the next month, the delegates to the Mississippi Secession
Convention reaffirmed that figure. In their "Declaration of . . .
Immediate Causes," drafted to explain their decision to abandon
the Union, the Mississippians wrote, "Our position is thoroughly
identified with the institution of slavery—the greatest material interest of the world." How great was that "material interest"? They
provided the answer at the conclusion of their "Declaration": "We
must either submit to degradation, and to the loss of property
worth four billions of money, or we must secede from the Union
framed by our fathers, to secure this as well as every other species
of property."[8]

Evidence generated on the floors of Richmond's slave-trading
firms certainly confirms the incredible wealth represented by this
"species of property."

We saw earlier in our detailed discussion of the Betts & Gregory price circular the astonishing dollar value the Richmond market placed on slave men, women, and children in the summer of
1860. What is equally astounding are the sums of money passing
through Richmond's slave auctions and showrooms on the eve of
the Civil War.

Press reports in the late antebellum years occasionally provided
a glimpse into the monetary dimensions of the trade. It is surprising that these chest-thumping declarations describing ever-rising
prices and escalating profits did not occur more often. Perhaps
white southerners did not want to trumpet this information too
loudly as sectional tension over the spread of slavery into the

western territories mounted in the 1850s. During these years, antislavery voices in the North increasingly pointed to a vast and incredibly wealthy "slave power conspiracy" to dominate American political and economic life. Why give these crazed abolitionists additional grist for their insane mill? But every now and then, the curtain lifted.

Probably the most detailed single report occurred when the editor of the *Warrenton (Virginia) Whig* toured the Richmond slave district in January 1857 and talked to some of the major traders. The principals at Dickinson, Hill & Co. reported "that the gross amount of their sales of negroes last year [1856] reached the enormous sum of two million dollars!" The Warrenton editor went on to say, "The entire sales of other houses of a similar kind in Richmond would make the amount go over four millions, and still the business is increasing." To support these figures, the wide-eyed visitor from Warrenton offered this anecdotal evidence: "We ourselves, witnessed the sale of 35 servants at an average of $700," and "Negro girls, not 10 years of age, sold for $800."[9]

This January 1857 press report, as staggering as it may seem at first glance (Dickinson, Hill & Co.'s report of sales worth $2 million in 1856 would translate into almost $58 million in today's purchasing power), may well have *underestimated* the value of Richmond's slave trade during this time frame. There is a single manuscript source, the sales records for a single slave dealer, Hector Davis, that points to exactly this conclusion: $2 million for a single firm, $4 million for the entire Richmond trade, may well have undershot the mark, and by a substantial margin.

In 1857, Hector Davis was operating one of the largest slave-trading firms in the city. At the age of thirty in 1846, he had moved to Richmond, apparently from nearby Goochland County, and established himself as an "auctioneer." His principal enterprise, however, was the operation of a slave jail, where enslaved men, women, and children were kept before sale.[10] This activity led directly to his establishing himself as a slave trader, as his advertisements in Richmond business directories during the 1850s made clear:

Hector Davis
Auctioneer & Commission Merchant
For the Sale of Negroes,
Franklin Street,
Richmond, VA.

Sells Negroes both publicly and privately,
and pledges his best efforts to obtain the highest market prices.
He has a safe and commodious jail, where he will board all
Negroes intended for his sales at 30 cents per day.[11]

The extent of Davis's business success is reflected not only in these advertisements but also by the fact that in February 1860 he and thirteen others, among them several of the city's major slave dealers, were able to charter their own bank. They called their financial institution the Traders Bank of the City of Richmond, and their state charter authorized a capital stock of "not . . . less than four hundred thousand dollars nor more than one million dollars." Hector Davis served as the president of the Traders Bank.[12]

In 2008 I had gone to do archival work at the Chicago History Museum on the papers of several Richmond slave dealers, and while I was there I saw a reference to two bound volumes described as Hector Davis & Co., Slave Sales Record Books. The archival staff offered to bring me a microfilm copy, but when I asked if I might examine the originals, they graciously agreed to let me do so. I am very grateful to them for doing this. I am not at all sure I would have had the patience to go through the microfilm as carefully as I did the pages of the original volumes.[13]

Volume 1 recorded the sales of Hector Davis & Co. from June 4, 1857, to April 14, 1860; volume 2 covered April 18, 1860, to January 7, 1865. It soon became evident that weekly sales figures had been put down, and that with a bit of patience and attention to detail, the totality of Davis's slave sales could be recorded: weekly, monthly, quarterly, and annual sales figures could be compiled. And that is exactly what I set out to do.

The scope of the trade revealed in these two volumes was astonishing. I remember turning over a page in volume 2 and seeing the following entry, one that filled an entire page of this oversized account book:

Sept. 27, 1860
To N. M. Lee & Co. for Purchase of 94 Negroes.

N. M. Lee & Co. was a Richmond slave-trading firm, and Davis and Lee had gone into partnership to assemble a "shipping parcel" for the New Orleans market. There followed a listing, first name only and price, of the men and women who made up this "lot":

George $1450	William $1360	Isaac $1470
Robert $1565	Henry $1425	Eliza $1455
Charity $1350	Violette $1320	Mary Ann $1465
Nancy $1485	Alcey $1310	Mary $1400

Line after line exactly like these, thirty-one lines in all, three names to a line, concluding with a single entry on the final line:

Harriet $1400.

(I have wondered if this Harriet might be the same woman John W. Abrams of Buckingham County, Virginia, was so anxious to sell to James Brady in 1852. Unlikely, surely, but the thought did cross my mind.)

The names of fifty-two adult women and forty-two adult men

make up this list. These ninety-four human beings sold in New Orleans for $128,300 (again, multiply that by approximately 29 to get today's valuation, just over $3.7 million).[14]

To repeat, every name is an adult man or woman. There is not a single child. The destruction of families involved in assembling this "shipping parcel" must have been devastating. And this is just one page from one Richmond slave trader's sales record book.

As Hector Davis & Co.'s monthly, quarterly, and annual sales figures emerged, the full extent of Richmond's slave trade in the years leading up to the Civil War became clear to me. The monetary value of this firm's sales turned out to be jaw-dropping, but they did not start out that way.

The 1857 figures were incomplete—the first recorded sales did not occur until June 4 of that year—and then in August, the failure of the Ohio Life Insurance & Trust Co. in Cincinnati triggered a financial panic that was reflected in the sharp drop-off in the firm's sales in the fourth quarter of 1857. Third-quarter sales had stood at $317,780; fourth-quarter sales fell to $52,115.

Recovery came quickly in 1858, however, as the following figures make clear:

HECTOR DAVIS & CO., SLAVE SALES, 1858
1st quarter $350,847
2nd quarter $307,129
3rd quarter $343,083
4th quarter $772,192

Total slave sales for 1858: $1,773,251

The next year, 1859, sales skyrocketed:

HECTOR DAVIS & CO., SLAVE SALES, 1859
1st quarter $838,460
2nd quarter $371,000

3rd quarter $675,110

4th quarter $787,002

Total slave sales for 1859: $2,671,572 (!)

To repeat, these are the sales figures for *one* firm in the city, and Hector Davis & Co. was not the largest slave-trading house; that dubious distinction belonged to Dickinson, Hill & Co. If the latter firm grossed $2 million in 1856, as the Warrenton newspaper editor reported, it would easily have topped that figure in the boom times of 1859. Adding in the sales of the likes of Betts & Gregory, Pulliam & Co., Davis Dupree & Co., N. M. Lee & Co., Browning, Moore & Co., and the numerous other firms that advertised daily sales in the Richmond press (think back to the partial list of advertisements at the end of chap. 4), not to mention the smaller firms that did not even bother to place such ads, slave sales in Richmond alone—a single Upper South city—in 1859 could easily have topped $7 million or $8 million. Capitalizing the Traders Bank of the City of Richmond early in 1860 would have presented no difficulty whatsoever to these affluent businessmen. They were, essentially, rolling in money.

The first quarter of that year brought even more success, spectacular success, to Hector Davis & Co. First-quarter slave sales in 1860 almost rocketed past an unbelievable milestone: the total was $983,907, just shy of $1 million for three months' sales. Buyers and sellers were practically beating down the doors of Hector Davis's handsome auction house.

The prosperity of the firm was reflected in the imposing physical layout of his trading facility on fashionable Franklin Street, in the heart of Richmond's business district: a three-story building sporting a bell tower and two interior balconies, and an auction floor measuring some fifty by one hundred feet. Two of the city's best hotels, the Exchange and the Ballard, were immediately adjacent to Davis's impressive building.[15] The man from Goochland

County who had come to Richmond fourteen years earlier had struck it rich in Virginia's capital city.

So had Betts & Gregory, Auctioneers. Although not quite in Hector Davis's league, this firm had certainly established a reputation as one of Richmond's premier long-distance traders. Deep South buyers—planters and slave dealers—were the lifeblood of their business. And, as is often the case when a boom is underway, optimism reigned, long past the point where caution was warranted.

As pointed out earlier, the Republican National Convention meeting in Chicago in May 1860 had chosen Abraham Lincoln as the party's presidential candidate, and that same month, the national Democratic Party had marked itself for electoral destruction in the upcoming fall campaign by splitting into irreconcilable North-South wings. The northern Democrats subsequently gathered in Baltimore in mid-June and nominated Stephen A. Douglas of Illinois as their presidential candidate. The southern Democrats, after first meeting in Richmond in early June, reassembled in Baltimore at the end of the month and nominated John C. Breckinridge of Kentucky to carry the banner of southern Democracy into the critical presidential election in November.

Any thinking white person in the slaveholding South should have taken note of these dire developments: Democrats divided, Republicans united, and the very real prospect of an electoral victory by a candidate, and a political party, committed to prohibiting the spread of slavery into the western territories. Since white southerners almost to a man (and a woman) believed that Abraham Lincoln was a closet abolitionist who would lay siege to the South and slavery once elected, optimism concerning the market for slave merchandise should have been hard to find on the trading floors of Richmond as July rolled around. But such was not the case at Betts & Gregory, Auctioneers.

A Betts & Gregory price circular that went out on July 20,

1860, reported prices virtually identical to those recorded on the August 2 list of prices current, the market report discussed at length in chapter 4:

Extra Men, $1,550 to $1,625.

No. 1 Men, $1,450 to $1,550.

Extra Girls, $1,375 to $1,450.

No. 1 Girls, $1,300 to $1,350.

The only significant addition to the Boys and Girls priced by height category was the handwritten insertion of the word "Good" before each of the price categories:

Good Boys 4 feet high, $575 to $675.

Good Boys 4 feet 3 inches high, $675 to $775.

Good Boys 4 feet 6 inches high, $850 to $950.

Good Boys 4 feet 9 inches high, $1,000 to $1,150.

Good Boys 5 feet high, $1,150 to $1,275.

Good Girls of same height as boys about the same prices.

The "Good Young Woman and first child" price was given as $1,250 to $1,450—again, almost exactly the same as the August 2, 1860, circular would report (the lower estimate in the August 2 report, $1,300, was actually *higher* than the one given on July 20).

What is striking about this July 20 prices current document is the handwritten market report at the end: "Good negroes are selling readily at the above figures; but inferior ones are rather dull." Betts & Gregory advised the person to whom this circular was sent—apparently a dealer or an agent—to get cracking: "Now is the time to buy good ones & bring them in. Hoping to see you soon, with a good lot."[16]

But all was not well, as Betts & Gregory were forced to acknowledge very soon. The firm's August 1, 1860, circular, modified the next day to reflect a deteriorating market, admitted, "The market is dull this week owing to the fact that there are but few Southern buyers in the market."

By the end of the month, reality had fully set in.

From Dickinson, Hill & Co. on August 25: "Our market is still dull, but very few No. 1 Negroes offering. 2nd & 3d rate hard to sell, and but very few buyers now here."[17]

From Betts & Gregory three days later: "The negro market is as dull as it could possibly be. Nothing selling and no prospect of selling anything." And Betts & Gregory issued firm instructions to one of their field agents in this August 28 letter: "Dont buy until you here from us which will be when a change takes place in the market."[18]

On November 6, 1860, the election of Abraham Lincoln as the sixteenth president of the United States sent shock waves reverberating across the South and plunged the Richmond slave market into near panic mode. "The election excitement is very intense and doubtless is the cause of the extreme flatness and inactivity of the present and past state of the market," Betts & Gregory reported on November 9. "There has been nothing doing for the last two or three weeks." The partners reported that "an extra No. 1 man" had sold on that day for $1,325 (some $300 less than the top price in the August 2 circular), but they added that "we do not regard it as an index of future sales as it is doubtless [i.e., doubtful] whether that price can be sustained in the future." Their closing promise to "write . . . when the excitement has subsided, or of any change in the market" seemed half-hearted at best.[19]

Hector Davis must have been feeling exactly the same way. As noted earlier, in the flush times during the first three months of 1860, his house had achieved $983,907 in slave sales; during the last quarter of 1860, total sales plummeted to $107,255, a falloff of over 90 percent.

On December 28, 1860, Dickinson, Hill & Co., Auctioneers, sent out something close to an epitaph for the halcyon days of the ever-rising Richmond slave market. The guidance of this firm—the city's largest slave trader—commanded close attention, and it was only appropriate that the partners resorted to a detailed printed broadside to notify their many customers of what the future might bring.

"The year is about to close and it will be difficult for us to say what will be done the ensuing year," they began. To compound the uncertainty, the partners admitted that they had "no hope for any political change which will give peace and confidence in commercial matters." They also conceded that something close to an out-of-control bubble had sent prices soaring in the past, a frank recognition of a reality most Richmond slave dealers had refused to acknowledge as late as the summer of 1860. "The speculations and extravagancies of the last three years have put up the prices of lands, negroes, and crops, to such a height that it could not be maintained, and the credit of the country has been extended to a degree unparalleled in this country before." Indeed, "the wealthiest men in the country are indebted to the Banks; and even those who lend out money are now borrowers, having vested more than their [own] money in lands, negroes, and stocks."

So what lay ahead in their market, the market that really mattered? "We think for some years to come negroes will not command over $1,000 for best men, and $800 for women" (a glance back at Betts & Gregory's August 2, 1860, circular will demonstrate just how much prices had collapsed). And things were only going to get worse. "During the incoming year we ought not to expect more than $800 for men, and $600 for women," and the partners feared "that even those prices will not be obtained for two or three months to come." To underline this last point, Dickinson, Hill & Co. closed with the disappointing admission, "Very few sales have been made this month, and those below these figures."[20]

As the North-South crisis escalated and neared a flash point over the continued Federal occupation of Fort Sumter in Charleston harbor, something akin to panic seemed to engulf some Virginia slave owners. Those who had obviously been counting on turning over some of their "good stock" in the inflated market of late 1859 and early 1860 bombarded Betts & Gregory with letters and, increasingly, frantic telegrams.

"Give me some idea what I could get for a good Girl 13 years old one 12 years old and a boy 10 years old or whether there would be any certainty of my selling them at all," a man named V. O. Witcher wrote Betts & Gregory on February 22, 1861.[21]

J. R. Sanders of Speedwell, Wythe County, in faraway Southwest Virginia, instructed Betts & Gregory on February 25, 1861, to "write by first mail" with "the prices [of] boys, Girls and men of the first order young & likely." Why? "I want to sell from 10 to 20."

Is this "a good time to sell or had I better wait longer," E. P. Crenshaw of Bacon's Castle, Surry County, Virginia, asked Betts & Gregory on March 4, 1861. He had "a negro man . . . from 33 to 35 years old, quite Black and healthy, and a good teamster" he wished to dispose of.

Via telegram, March 30, 1861, from Parr & Farish, Culpeper Court House, Virginia, to Betts & Gregory, Richmond: "Is there any change in the Negro market—answer immediately."

Another telegram, this one from Bolling & Bro., Wytheville, Virginia, March 31, 1861, to Betts & Gregory, Richmond: "How are negroes selling answer immediately."

But Betts & Gregory were facing their own crisis. They had borrowed heavily from one of the mainstays of the local slave trade, the Farmers' Bank of Richmond, and William H. Macfarland, the president of that bank (as well as of the Richmond & Petersburg Railroad), was threatening to call in their outstanding loans as their notes fell due on March 1.

"I rec'd. yours this morning dated the 17th & contents noted," William H. Betts wrote his partner, Jack Gregory, on February 20, 1861. "I will write a letter to Mr. Macfarland and send to you to hand to him," he went on. "I think the Bank will renew with us," he noted, and besides, "if they will not . . . we cant help it. We will not be the first that have not met their liabilities at maturity." Betts thought his partner was giving up "two easy," and added that "if we are protested that . . . is no criminal offence, and I suppose we can get on just the same as others do."[22]

William Betts's apparent optimism was totally unwarranted. The collapsing Richmond slave market dragged Betts & Gregory under. The *Richmond Enquirer* reported on April 18, 1861, that another Richmond slave dealer, E. H. Stokes, had bought them out and taken over their Franklin Street facilities. Promising to "give strict attention to both public and private sales," Stokes was soon running ads in the Richmond press and inviting prospective buyers and sellers to his "New Auction House for the Sale of Negroes" located on Franklin Street, "3rd door below 15th."[23]

The Richmond slave-trading community clearly saw their future imperiled as the great Secession Winter of 1860–61 unfolded. Not only was there a financial crisis raging, seven states of the Deep South, beginning with South Carolina on December 20, 1860, and concluding with Texas on February 1, 1861, had seceded from the Union, raising the very real prospect of war. Where would Virginia stand? The traders seem to have done everything they could to push the commonwealth into the Confederate camp.

When the Virginia State Convention assembled in Richmond in February 1861 to decide the question of Union or secession, the slave traders appear to have thrown their still considerable wealth into the battle.

Samuel McDowell Moore, a lawyer from the Valley town of Lexington and a strong Unionist delegate to the convention, told fellow Lexington lawyer James D. Davidson in late March that Richmond's "negro traders" were "buying up most of the presses in the State" to silence antisecessionist voices.[24] "Every newspaper in the City is against us," he added in a subsequent letter, and he again traced the origins of this drumbeat for disunion to the same source. "The most of the difficulties we have to contend with, arise from the powerful influence exerted by the most potent money power, that ever has existed in Virginia," he wrote Davidson in early April. "I mean the power of the Traders in negroes."[25]

Moore's indictment of "the Traders in negroes" was searing. "They own a Bank in this City, and have millions of money under their control." He added that reports circulating in Richmond "said that the profits of one trader here, in the last year, were over a hundred thousand dollars." And there was no question where the traders stood in the escalating sectional crisis. "The interest of these people is entirely with the seceded states, and to promote it, they would sacrifice every other interest in the state, without the least scruple."

Moore had no doubt that the slave traders "are spending their money freely, in order to influence the public mind in favor of immediate secession." He claimed it was a well-known fact in Richmond "that the mobs gotten up here to parade the streets, and insult Union men in the Convention, was gotten up by them."

Samuel McDowell Moore's description of the power, wealth, and influence of Richmond's slave traders was no exaggeration. These men still controlled staggering sums of money. And the chance that Virginia might remain in the Union, with dire consequences for their lucrative human commerce with the Deep South, was a threat, as Moore described it, that they obviously took with dead seriousness.

The firing on Fort Sumter on April 12, 1861, and Lincoln's subsequent call for troops decided Virginia's fate. Richmond's slave traders got their wish, but short-term success turned into long-term disaster. Virginia's secession, the move they hoped would salvage their business and sustain their trading empire, placed the commonwealth squarely in the crosshairs of the bloodiest war the Western Hemisphere had ever seen.

Slave trading would continue in Virginia's capital city for four more years, but the falloff was dramatic. The 1861 sales of Hector

Davis & Co. from April to the end of the year demonstrated just how dramatic that decline had been:

HECTOR DAVIS & CO., SLAVE SALES, 1861
2nd quarter $60,545
3rd quarter $17,555
4th quarter $26,975

The final slave sale, in highly inflated Confederate currency, that I uncovered in my archival searches took place in January 1865, almost three months to the day before Virginia's capital city fell to Federal forces:

Richmond Jan. 7, 1865
$7,000
    At sight pay to S. H. E. Deupree
    Seven thousand dollars for the purchase of one
1 Bay Horse at $2000 & girl Maria at $5000
                R. H. Davis
To Messrs Hill Dickinson & Co.[26]

On the reverse of this document are four words that seemed to sum up, as well as anything I encountered in all the time I was researching this project, the dehumanizing essence of the Old South's slave trade, the absolute inner core of this dismal traffic—the chattel principal, the commodification of human beings, the turning of men, women, and children into the equivalent of livestock.

This line, on the back of this last sale, reads:

Bill for Horse & Girl

In Conclusion

Why do the grown-ups put so much hate in the children?

During the days of late February 1861, as the Richmond firm of
Betts & Gregory, Auctioneers, was facing financial ruin, William
H. Betts was out of town. He was at his home in Abingdon in far
Southwest Virginia, over three hundred miles from Richmond,
and he would not leave. "My children all have the measles," he
wrote his partner on February 20, "but my wife hasn't taken it
yet," and under these circumstances, there was no way he was going to abandon his family. Even as his business was collapsing in
Richmond, his wife, facing the prospect of serious illness, and his
children, already ill, came first.[1]

Betts made the same point in a frantic letter to William Macfarland, the president of the Farmers' Bank of Richmond, written
on the same day. "I received a letter this morning from my Partner Mr. Gregory saying that we had some notes due about the 1st
of March if he should fail to make collection [for previous slave
sales], which I fear he will do," Betts told Macfarland. "You must
renew with us don't let us be protested," he pleaded. "I would come
down my self but the situation of my family is such that I cant
leave," he explained, in an obvious appeal for sympathy; "four of
my children has just had the measles, and I am looking every day
for my wife to have it."[2]

Sickness comes up often in the correspondence of slave traders, but invariably in a dramatically different context. Joseph Pointer sent three slave men to R. H. Dickinson in Richmond in February 1846 for whom he and his partners had paid top dollar, and in consequence, he wanted them well looked after. All three were confined at Robert Lumpkin's jail awaiting sale. "Ask Mr. Lumpkin to see that the negroes wash & fix up as well as they can for the market," Pointer instructed Dickinson. "Say to Mr. Lumpkin that we wish him to be careful to keep them from the small pox & measels."[3]

The contrast between these two circumstances—Betts in 1861, Joseph Pointer in 1846—could not be more stark. Betts was concerned for his wife and children, even to the point of seeing his business possibly go under; Pointer was concerned for one thing and one thing only, his bottom line. His investment had been made at "verry high" cost, he told Dickinson, and every care should be taken to ensure that he and his partners did not suffer pecuniary loss.

The chattel principle drove everything before it. One reads through the correspondence of slave traders with astonishment and an appalled recognition of the lengths to which antebellum white southerners—my people—would go in order to profit from this traffic in human beings. Over and over again, man's inhumanity to man is writ large in these letters.

From Dickinson, Hill & Co., Richmond, December 20, 1858, to Joseph Dickinson, on successive lines of a market report:

No. 1 Woman & Child 1250 to 1350
Families rather dull and hard to sell.[4]

Or this. From W. S. Mallicote, Yorktown, Virginia, to Betts & Gregory, Richmond, February 22, 1861:

[A] Gentleman of my acquaintance has some negroes he

wishes to sell . . . he is an old man and says he wants to sell them before he dies.[5]

Or this. From Thomas H. Lipscomb, Fredericksburg, to Browning, Moore & Co., Richmond, July 31, 1860:

Mr. Wallace says you will please dispose of his servants to the best advantage, provided they will nett Seventeen Hundred & fifty or Eighteen Hundred dollars.

If you think they will bring more you can sell the two largest children separately.[6]

Or this. From P. N. Dulin, Smith Grove, North Carolina, to Betts & Gregory, Richmond, May 25, 1861:

I write you this to ascertain the price of negroes in Richmond at this time. I want to buy 5 or 6 boys and girls from 8 to 12 years old or, from 5½ feet to 4½ feet high. You will please answer this and inform me whether I can get them in Richmond and at what price.[7]

Or this via telegram:

American Telegraph Company
    Received Richmond, Virginia, 12 o'clock 46 minutes, February 15, 1860, from J. O. Stanfield, Lynchburg, Virginia.
    To Browning, Moore & Co.
    What can be had for Two (2) Girls Number One. One about Seven (7) the other Nine—[8]

The examples could go on and on. The world represented by Betts & Gregory's August 2, 1860, market report, the document that started me off on this bleak journey, that world of "Extra Men" and "Extra Girls," of "Second rate or ordinary" adult males and adult females, of boys and girls sold by height, of "Good young woman & first child," was a world capable of generating a seemingly infinite number of cruel and outrageous acts.

Once again, we turn to that all-important question: how can we explain white southerners' ready acceptance of all this? How can we explain this ongoing, day-after-day indifference to obvious human suffering? How can we begin to comprehend the level of casually dispensed cruelty that was on display every day in the slave South and that apparently almost no white people saw? Part of the answer is assuredly greed—pure, simple, unadulterated avarice. There was an ocean of money sloshing around in the cesspool that was the Old South's slave system. And of course white southerners were looking to get their share. It mattered not that this money (certainly from our point of view) carried with it the stench of that foul receptacle that was human bondage.

Greed will help explain the following extraordinary document, but it does not tell us anything like the whole story.

The dehumanizing nature of the chattel principle was never more clearly demonstrated to me than in a manuscript letter I came across when I was doing the research for my second major project, the one that took book form in *Bond of Iron*. In dealing with ironmaster William Weaver's family members who had come down from Pennsylvania over the years to help him manage his various installations in the Valley of Virginia, I ran across a letter written in 1858 by the wife of one of his nephews, a Virginia woman by the name of Ann Overton Dickinson Davis. Ann Davis's mother had died intestate, and there was every chance that her mother's slave property would be distributed widely among family members. Ann Dickinson Davis was trying to prevent such a distribution, and her letter pleading with her husband, William Davis, to intervene is both remarkable and stunningly revealing.

Ann Davis had earlier helped to raise nine slave children belonging to the family, and she named each of them in case her husband had forgotten: Jenny, Nelson, Emily, Frankey, Kate, Edgar, Albert, Allen ("the boy who was killed by the horse"), and "poor Margarette who was small when we got her." Her investment of time, energy, and effort should count for something, she insisted, when the fate of these slave children was decided. "I nursed them when sick," she wrote. "I saw that there Clothes were washed and I pached [patched] for them with my own hands yes I have pached for Jenny just before I left to keep her from suffering."

Then Ann Davis went on to say this. "I had to act as a Mother even in giving them a piece of bread when hungry yes many & many a time I gave Nelson something to eate when I gave my own." And then she added a remarkable sentence. "Children must be attended to white or black. . . ." Finally, a spark of genuine humanity! At long last, a lifting of the dark veil of slavery, I thought. I felt like shouting "Hallelujah!" from my seat at the archives reading room table. And then I continued reading. I will quote this sentence in its entirety: "Children must be attended to white or black and now I want to ask you why *I did it all.* Did you not tell me from your own lips that they were for our *Children* . . . did I not nurse Edgar with the fever when very low too low to be raised from the bead [bed] to the pot. . . . Yes Dear William I done it for my Children."[9]

Ann Dickinson Davis had transformed her maternal care and concern for these black children into what amounted to a product, to be dispensed as needed to ensure that these black boys and girls would survive and serve as an inheritance for her own children. She had turned motherhood itself into a commodity. Slavery had done this to Jenny, Nelson, Emily, Frankey, Kate, Edgar, Albert, Allen, and Margarette at birth. One would have to look under many archival rocks in the sordid manuscript history of slavery to find a more depressing illustration of the oppressive weight of slavery and race on the antebellum southern white mind. White motherhood corrupted by the chattel principle, just like black childhood—go back to those listings on Betts & Gregory's August 1860 market report for "Boys" and "Girls" starting at "4 feet high," or J. O. Stanfield's 1860 telegram, cited above, inquiring what he could expect to make on the sale of a seven-year-old and a nine-year-old girl.

My ancestors did more than coexist with this institution and draw monetary gain from it. They endorsed it, they embraced it, they celebrated it, they destroyed a hallowed political union to protect it, and they launched what turned out to be the most blood-drenched war in American history to defend it. And with racial segregation, my parents' generation, and my generation, did much the same thing—no secession and civil war this time around, but blood was shed over and over again as the terror of lynching gripped the South in the late nineteenth century and well into the twentieth. And the Jim Crow laws and institutions built by that turn-of-the-century generation, the generation of "Radical racism," were passed down as immutable folkways and endured into my own generation.

It is still not easy for us white southerners to come to grips with our collective blindness to these evils, but it seems to me that we must. So, then, how can we understand our inability, our refusal, to see slavery (and later racial segregation) for what it truly was?

I have an exercise that I ask the students in my History of the Old South course to undertake toward the end of the semester. It comes after we have spent weeks studying the institution of slavery and the impact of slavery on the society, the politics, the culture, the economy, and the mind of the antebellum South. I ask them to read two letters, two of the most powerful manuscripts I have come across in my archival searches. Their assignment is to go over these two documents very carefully, line by line, analyze their contents, and answer the following question: "Would antebellum white southerners experience guilt over slavery after reading what is written here? Or did they find ways to look the consequences of slavery in the face on a daily basis and experience no guilt over the South's 'peculiar institution'"?

I add that historians have debated this question vigorously for decades and have come down on both sides of the guilt question. Their task—my students' task—is to analyze the two primary documents in light of this question. Again, would antebellum white southerners familiar with the content of these two letters have experienced guilt over what is written here? Or would they have done just the opposite and experienced no guilt over what is described? My final comment to them is that there is no way to answer this question definitively, but we can try to understand white southern attitudes during this era and get some idea of how they saw the world in which they lived.

Since I am asking you, the reader, to take on a mental challenge identical to the one my students undertake, it will be necessary for me to present these documents in their entirety, with apologies for imposing two more block quotations on you. Both are in the manuscript collections in Alderman Library at the University of Virginia.

First, by way of introduction, an advertisement that appeared for a number of consecutive weeks in the *Lynchburg Virginian* in November and December 1826:

> EXECUTOR'S SALE—Will be sold on the premises, on the first day of January, 1827, that well known and valuable estate called Poplar Forest, lying in the counties of Bedford and Campbell, the property of Thomas Jefferson, dec. . . . also about 70 likely and valuable negroes, with stock, crops, &c.

This advertisement was signed "Thomas J. Randolph, Executor of Th. Jefferson, dec."[10]

Several days after the January 1, 1827, auction sale, a local man, whose son had purchased a Poplar Forest slave girl on his behalf, wrote the following letter to Thomas J. Randolph.[11] As will become clear, the buyer allowed the girl to remain at Poplar Forest for several days after the auction, and during that time something almost unimaginable happened:

Lynchburg, Jany. 11th. 1827.

Sir,

On Saturday & Sunday last, I sent my son . . . to inform you, that the girl named Jeanette, aged 14 years, which he bought last week at Poplar Forest for $290, is burned from the right shoulder to the foot, particularly her breast & she is so burned as to have but little use of her right arm & leg & of several fingers, which she cannot use. Dr. Cabell, who visited her, says that she will have a cancerous breast. She says that all this was caused by the Overseer, who, in an angry fit, threw her twice in the fire, which had caught accidently, to a stack of straw, from a fire that she & a little boy had lighted in the night, while they were feeding the cattle, for which purpose they had been sent. Mr. Payne visited her & he can state to you her situation. I informed her, that I should be obliged to send her back; she then implored me not to do it, for she would not find her mother, brothers & sisters & that he [the overseer] would punish her for having made public his treatment towards her.

I now propose you, Sir, if it meet your approbation to choose a gentleman & I shall name another, who will proceed together to estimate how much she is worth & I make you the offer to keep her at the price she will be valued by our joint appraisers. This is all I can do, being guided by humanity for the unhappy creature & being the most just offer I can make. I am willing to keep her to attend to my child, for she cannot do much else.

Expect[ing] your answer on this subject, I remain Yours,

P. H. Leuba

The second document I have my students read as part of this assignment is one of those rarest of antebellum southern manuscripts: a letter written by a slave, in this instance, a man living in Kentucky.[12] His future is hanging in the balance, and he is pleading with the woman in Virginia who has inherited him to do the right thing:

January eth 1854
Simpson County Ky

Dear Mistress

I embrace this opertunity of droping you a few lines of letting you know the troubles and misfortunes. I have lost two most excelent masters whitch seems like parting bone and sinew I am well at present hoping the[se] lines will find you all well My loving master rote to you concerning me but having an knowledge of his [approaching] death before he received your leter . . . he made other provisions for me I would be very glad to see you all and live with you if it was not fore my wife and child it apeares to me that it is more than I can bare to leave them tho I am black I have feeling becoming man and wife now I want to know what is the lest you will take for me I wa[n]t you to remember me as an obediant servant and it was Andrews request for me not to go out of the family now it is my choise to live with John R. McCrery him and Smith Sanders has ben good to us in our afflicktions John R. Mc-Crery has ben good to them I want him to by me on the account of my wife and if not I wold prefer living with you all again Johns famely is well and sends the best respects now on reseptions of this write to me and let me [k]now what is the terms

Eavans McCrery,
an obediant servant to Miss Elizabeth McCrery and Margaret G
Hararet Riten By me

Postscript Smith Sanders and John lives cloce together Sanders owns my wif they all sems glad for me to stay we are living in a helthy county James had beter health than he ever had and done more work

[This letter is addressed on the reverse to:]

Miss Elizabeth McCrery

Stoners Store Post [Office]

Roanoak Cty. Virginia

Again, my challenge to my students is relatively simple: guilt or no guilt? I repeat that there is no way we can be sure, but I want them to be thoughtful, write well, and support their answer by drawing on what they have learned thus far in the course.

The papers I receive in response to this charge are fascinating. Over the time I have assigned this topic, the responses have broken down roughly in a 50–50 split, approximately half say "guilt," about half say "no guilt."

The class discussion the day they turn in their papers is invariably one of the best of the semester. The students square off in a vigorous debate, fueled by the fact that, in the course of writing their essays, they have read and considered these letters closely and contextualized them in the light of what they have already learned about the antebellum South. Toward the end of class, it seems only fair that I should offer my take on the question I posed to them.

It probably will come as no surprise to learn that I come down heavily on the "no guilt" side of this divide. I start by examining the two documents and possible contemporary white response to their contents. I end up talking about my growing up in the Jim Crow South.

First, my take on the letter written by P. H. Leuba of Lynchburg to Jefferson's executor, Thomas J. Randolph. Despite the horrific events described in this document, it is essentially a business letter. Leuba is seeking a reduction in the price of the slave girl,

Jeanette, who is now "damaged goods"; she is not the same human merchandise purchased at Poplar Forest on New Year's Day, 1827. At no point is there any discussion of punishment for the overseer who committed this outrage. In the end, Leuba falls back on the stereotypical notion of the "good master" looking out for this lowly charge. Although he claims to be "guided by humanity" in his effort to help this "unhappy creature" (who has already been sold away from "her mother, brothers & sisters"), his altruism is dependent on "our joint appraisers" reaching a sufficiently reduced price. Once again, the chattel principle rears its ugly head. The best Jeanette—this young girl who is "burned from the right shoulder to the foot, particularly her breast" and "is so burned as to have but little use of her right arm & leg & of several fingers," with the prospect of a "cancerous breast" in her future—the best she can hope for is that Leuba will "keep her to attend to my child, for she cannot do much else." I see no guilt here over a system that would permit such an atrocity to occur. Only a gut-wrenching act of unspeakable cruelty to a black girl, and then two white men trying to set the issue "right" by reevaluating the worth of this piece of human property.

If Leuba's letter shows me no evidence of guilt, what about the possible contemporary white response to Eavans McCrery's extraordinary letter? Could Miss Elizabeth McCrery have read this document and not have experienced pangs of guilt over the position in which the institution of slavery has placed this man? Someone for whom the prospect of being separated from "my wife and child . . . is more than I can bare," someone who is even forced to plead that "tho I am black I have feeling becoming man and wife"? Would not some vestige of white guilt be spawned by these words and these circumstances? Not necessarily. Once again, there is the possibility that Elizabeth McCrery can simply play the role of the "good mistress" and accede to Eavans's request (but one suspects the price paid by the prospective owner in Kentucky would have to meet her expectations, or come very close to it). She could "do the right thing" by Eavans (just as my mother and father did the "right thing" by Illinois and Joe Culver when they helped them buy their own home) and never once have to confront the existence of the institution that placed this man in this intolerable circumstance in the first place. Along the way, Elizabeth McCrery could bask in the ego-warming notion that she had done her Christian duty by this lowly but humble servant who had been placed in her charge. A lowly, humble *black* servant.

And therein lies the key to this whole undertaking, everything this book is about: race. If you begin with the absolute belief in white supremacy—unquestioned white superiority/unquestioned black inferiority—everything falls neatly into place: the African is inferior racial "stock," living in sin and ignorance and barbarism and heathenism on the "Dark Continent" until enslaved by the English, the Spanish, the French, the Portuguese, the list goes on. Slavery thus miraculously becomes a form of "uplift" for this supposedly benighted and brutish race of people. And once notions of white supremacy and black inferiority are in place in the American South, they are passed on from one generation to the next with all the certainty and inevitability of a genetic trait. As Illinois so eloquently put it on that memorable drive home many years ago, "Charles, why do the grown-ups put so much hate in the children?" She knew whereof she spoke. She cut right to the heart of the matter, and I recognized it as soon as she said it. Nor can I improve on what she said. I lived it for the first seventeen years of my life: *Ezekiel,* the orange china used by Illinois and Ed, our two separate and grossly unequal bathrooms, Bill's approach to our home, *Eneas Africanus,* "The Peasel Tree Sermon," "Rastus and Lulabelle" jokes, my father's passionate embrace of, and my mother's quiet acquiescence in, Jim Crow. All these things and many, many more helped make me who I was—a Confederate youth, a son of the Jim Crow South, a racist. And I, we, virtually all of us, did not feel the slightest twinge of guilt about any of this. I know because I speak from my own experience. I lived this blissful, ignorant, guilt-free life on the white side of the color line the whole time I was growing up. I should not have, but I did, and this is the story I tell my students when they hand me their essays on the presence or absence of guilt over slavery in the Old South.

So we, generations of us, from Thomas Roderick Dew to Charles Burgess Dew, became blind to what was right in front of us—slavery in the nineteenth century, segregation in the twentieth. We see a black skin and all the assumptions we have been taught or learned, much of it simply by childhood observation ("osmosis" was the word I used earlier), kick in. And the system that elevates *us* and subordinates *them* seems right and proper and the way things were meant to be. The alternatives, abolition in the nineteenth century, integration in the twentieth century, we come to see as uncivilized, intolerable, unthinkable, an absolute nightmare, and we close ranks to keep the beast—our black "Sambo" corrupted by outside agitators and turned into a "Nat Turner" in the nineteenth century, the black male sexual predator in the twentieth—in his cage.

It is a sordid tale, all of this, spanning centuries and generations, but we are not doomed by it. We can do better, we have done better. But we must do better still. We have to shuck off the last vestiges of that reptilian skin of racism, even if we do not think we are still carrying it around. Because we are. And our failure to shed that skin will continue to poison our politics and shackle the South, and in many ways the rest of our country, with decades of continuing strife and racial injustice. We should strive to be, and we should become, the generation of "grown-ups" who finally, at long last, refuse to put the "hate in the children."

NOTES

ABBREVIATIONS

AAS   Manuscript Collections, American Antiquarian Society, Worcester, MA

CHM   Research Center, Chicago History Museum, Chicago, IL

DU   David M. Rubinstein Rare Book and Manuscripts Library, Duke University Library, Durham, NC

LC   Manuscript Division, Library of Congress, Washington, DC

SHSW   Archives, State Historical Society of Wisconsin Library, Madison, WI

UVA   Albert and Shirley Small Special Collections Library, University of Virginia Library, Charlottesville, VA

VHS   Library & Manuscripts Collection, Virginia Historical Society, Richmond, VA

INTRODUCTION

1. Thomas Roderick Dew, "Abolition of Negro Slavery," in Drew Gilpin Faust, ed., *The Ideology of Slavery: Proslavery Thought in the Antebellum South, 1830–1860* (Baton Rouge, LA, 1981), 31.

ONE: CONFEDERATE YOUTH

1. The family history that follows is based largely on the following sources: Dew Family Bible, in the author's possession; family oral tradition; "The St. Petersburg Dews," *St. Petersburg Times,* Mar. 19, 1967; and obituary notices for Roy Lane Dew, *St. Petersburg Times*, Nov. 9, 1962; R. Joseph Dew Sr., *St. Petersburg Times,* Dec. 21, 1964, and Jack Carlos Dew, *St. Petersburg Independent,* June 2, 1975.

2. There is a superb scholarly history of St. Petersburg: Raymond Arsenault, *St. Petersburg and the Florida Dream, 1888–1950* (Gainesville, FL, 1996).

3. Douglas Southall Freeman, *Lee's Lieutenants: A Study in Command*, 3 vols. (New York, 1946). These volumes are still on my bookshelf.

4. John S. Tilley, *Facts the Historians Leave Out: A Youth's Confederate Primer* (Montgomery, AL, 1951).

5. Ibid., 5, 11–14, 28–29, 31, 65–67, 69–71.

6. I still have this book and have used it frequently over the years: Sir Paul Harvey, ed., *The Oxford Companion to English Literature* (3rd ed. Oxford, 1953).

7. Benjamin P. Thomas, *Abraham Lincoln: A Biography* (New York, 1952), 188.

8. Richard Hofstadter, *The American Political Tradition and the Men Who Made It* (New York, 1948), 76.

TWO: THE MAKING OF A RACIST

1. Elvira Garner, *Ezekiel* (New York, 1937). Copy in author's possession; the pages in this book are unnumbered.

2. Lillian Smith, *Killers of the Dream* (New York, 1949).

3. Anne Moody, *Coming of Age in Mississippi* (New York, 1968).

4. W. E. Debnam, *Weep No More, My Lady* (Raleigh, NC, 1950), 9, 29, 40–43. The copyright page of the "1953 Edition" contains the information on the printing history to date and the statement "Copies printed thus far—210,000." This same 1953 copyright page also offered a "deluxe cloth bound edition" priced at $2.00. "The deluxe edition is a handsome little book," the author promised, with a cover of "Confederate grey" and "the Confederate battle flag . . . stamped in gold" on the front.

5. Stephen Kantrowitz, *Ben Tillman & the Reconstruction of White Supremacy* (Chapel Hill, NC, 2000), 241.

6. W. J. Cash, *The Mind of the South* (1941; repr. New York, 1991), 54. U.S. senator Benjamin Ryan ("Pitchfork Ben") Tillman of South Carolina used almost identical language in 1911 when he referred to "the complaisance of the negro women." See Kantrowitz, *Ben Tillman*, 241.

7. See my *Apostles of Disunion: Southern Secession Commissioners and the Causes of the Civil War* (Charlottesville, VA, 2001), and my essay "Lincoln, the Collapse of Deep South Moderation, and the

Triumph of Secession: A South Carolina Congressman's Moment of Truth," in Don H. Doyle, ed., *Secession as an International Phenomenon: From America's Civil War to Contemporary Separatist Movements* (Athens, GA, 2010), 97–114.

8. Thomas Jefferson, *Notes on the State of Virginia* (1785; repr. New York, 1964), 139.

9. Quoted in Percy Lee Rainwater, *Mississippi: Storm Center of Secession* (Baton Rouge, LA, 1938), 147–48.

10. Quoted in Dewey W. Grantham, *The South in Modern America: A Region at Odds* (New York, 1994), 195.

11. John Bell Williams, "Civil Rights," *Speakers Magazine,* March 1949, 8–10.

12. Quoted in Dan T. Carter, *From George Wallace to Newt Gingrich: Race in the Conservative Counterrevolution, 1963–1994* (Baton Rouge, LA, 1996), 3.

13. Edward L. Ayers, *The Promise of the New South: Life after Reconstruction* (New York, 1992), 432.

14. Debnam, *Weep No More, My Lady,* 53, 57.

15. See Joel Williamson, *The Crucible of Race: Black-White Relations in the American South since Emancipation* (New York, 1984).

16. Ibid.

17. T. R. Dew, "Abolition of Negro Slavery," in Faust, ed., *Ideology of Slavery,* 38, 66. Like many white southerners before and after, Dew warned sternly against "a commingling of the races," a disaster that would reduce "civilized man to the level of barbarism" and end "the mighty work of civilization" (47).

18. Harry Stillwell Edwards, *Eneas Africanus* (Macon, GA, 1920), 5.

19. Ibid., 7–14.

20. Ibid., 38–47.

21. For background on WLAC, see John Egerton, *Speak Now against the Day: The Generation before the Civil Rights Movement in the South* (New York, 1994), 245, 538.

THREE: THE UNMAKING OF A RACIST

1. Numan V. Bartley, *The New South, 1945–1980* (Baton Rouge, LA, 1995), 199–206.

2. See John W. Chandler, *The Rise and Fall of Fraternities at Williams College: Clashing Cultures and the Transformation of a Liberal Arts College* (Williamston, MA, 2014), 76–77.

3. "Robert C. L. Scott," Faculty & Staff Biographical File, Williams College Archives & Special Collections, Williamstown, MA.

4. C. Vann Woodward, *Origins of the New South, 1877–1913* (Baton Rouge, LA, 1951).

5. Manuscript in author's possession.

FOUR: THE DOCUMENT

1. Broadside in the Chapin Library, Williams College, Williamstown, MA.

2. U.S. Customs Service Records: Port of New Orleans, LA, Inward Slave Manifests, 1807–1860, microfilm, 12 reels, Scholarly Resources (Wilmington, DE, 1996).

3. www.measuringworth.com, accessed January 24, 2015.

4. "Hannibal Hamlin," *Montgomery (AL) Weekly Mail,* Nov. 9, 1860, and "Pedigree of Hannibal Hamlin," *Charleston (SC) Mercury,* Jan. 22, 1861. The quotation is from the *Charleston Mercury.*

5. See advertisements under "Auction Sales," *Richmond Enquirer* and *Richmond Whig and Public Advertiser,* June, July, August, 1860.

FIVE: THE CORRESPONDENCE, PART I

1. Henry L. Swint, ed., *Dear Ones at Home: Letters from Contraband Camps* (Nashville, TN, 1966), 4–6.

2. Lucy Chase Papers, and Slavery in the United States Collection, 1703–1905, AAS; Cornelius Chase Family Papers, LC.

3. Thomas Williams to R. H. Dickinson, May 26, 1847, Slavery in the United States Collection, AAS. All citations to this correspondence are from this collection.

4. Thomas Williams to R. H. Dickinson, June 3, 1847.

5. The Campbell firm is discussed in Frederic Bancroft, *Slave Trading in the Old South* (1931; repr. New York, 1959), 25, 121, 316–17.

6. W. L. Campbell to R. H. Dickinson, June 20, 1847, Slavery in the U.S. Collection, AAS.

7. John S. Campbell to R. H. Dickinson, Aug. 5, 1848, ibid.

8. Carter L. Campbell to Mr. Dickinson, Aug. 15, 1848, ibid.
9. See Eugene D. Genovese, *Roll, Jordan, Roll: The World the Slaves Made* (New York, 1974), 75–86.
10. B. M. Campbell to R. H. Dickinson, July 11, 1849, Richard H. Dickinson Papers, CHM.
11. B. M. Campbell to R. H. Dickinson, Feb. 16, 1850, ibid
12. W. H. Betts to "Dear Edward," Dec. 28, 1859, Cornelius Chase Family Papers, LC.
13. W. H. Betts to "Dear Edward," Dec. 31, 1859, Slavery in the U.S. Collection, AAS.
14. Daniel R. Hundley, *Social Relations in Our Southern States* (1860; repr. Baton Rouge, LA, 1979), 140–41.
15. Gregg D. Kimball, *American City, Southern Place: A Cultural History of Antebellum Richmond* (Athens, GA, 2000), 112.
16. Tabb Carter to R. H. Dickinson, Aug. 1, 1848, Slavery in the U.S. Collection, AAS. All subsequent letters cited in this chapter are from this collection.

SIX: THE CORRESPONDENCE, PART II

1. C. B. Ackiss to Browning, Moore & Co., July 3, 1860, Cornelius Chase Family Papers, LC.
2. Sidnum Grady to James Brady, June 23, 1846, James Brady Papers, UVA.
3. Hodges, Ray & Pulliam to James Brady, March 14, 1847, ibid.
4. Hodges, Ray & Pulliam to James Brady, May 24, 1847, ibid.
5. Pulliam & Slade to James Brady, Oct. 30, 1850, ibid.
6. Pulliam & Davis to James Brady, Sept. 26, Oct. 13, 1854, ibid.
7. Pulliam & Davis to James Brady, Nov. 21, 1854, ibid.
8. Dickinson, Hill & Co. to James Brady, May 21, 1855, ibid.
9. Maria Perkins to Richard Perkins, Oct. 8, 1852, in Willie Lee Rose, ed., *A Documentary History of Slavery in North America* (New York, 1976), 151.
10. Charles E. Beveridge and Charles C. McLaughlin, eds., *The Papers of Frederick Law Olmsted,* vol. 2, *Slavery in the South* (Baltimore, MD, 1981), 250, 255.
11. Edm'd. Pate to Callohill Mennis, March 30, 1828, Edmund Pate Letter, VHS.

12. Edmund C. Fitzhugh and Alex Fitzhugh to R.H. Dickinson, Feb. 16, 1846, Slavery in the U.S. Collection, AAS.

13. James M. Pelby to R. H. Dickinson, Feb. 23, 1846, ibid.

14. John G. Skelton to R. H. Dickinson [Feb. 1846], ibid.

15. S. C. Pender to R. H. Dickinson & Bro., Feb. 8, 1846, ibid.

16. S. C. Pender to R. H. Dickinson & Bro., Feb. 27, 1846, ibid.

17. N. C. Trowbridge to R. H. Dickinson & Bro., March 14, 1850, ibid.

18. N. C. Trowbridge to R. H. Dickinson, April 6, 1850, Richard H. Dickinson Papers, CHM.

19. W. B. Newton to Dickinson, Hill & Co., Feb. 17, 1857, Slavery in the U.S. Collection, AAS.

20. L. Wilkes to Dickinson, Hill & Co., July 11, 1855, Richard H. Dickinson Papers, CHM.

21. Wm. E. Cocke Jr., to Dickinson & Hill, Oct. 15, 1860, ibid.

22. J. Hobbs to R. H. Dickinson & Bro., Feb. 17, 1846, Slavery in the U.S. Collection, AAS.

23. John W. Abrams to Jas. Brady, Esq., July 20, 1852, James Brady Papers, UVA.

24. J. W. Mason to Dickinson, Hill & Co., Feb. 28, 1857, Slavery in the U.S. Collection, AAS.

SEVEN: THE MARKET

1. Ira Berlin, *Generations of Captivity: A History of African-American Slaves* (Cambridge, MA, 2003), 161.

2. Michael Tadman, *Speculators and Slaves: Masters, Traders, and Slaves in the Old South* (Madison, WI, 1989), 44.

3. Berlin, *Generations of Captivity*, 168.

4. James L. Huston, *Calculating the Value of the Union: Slavery, Property Rights, and the Economic Origins of the Civil War* (Chapel Hill, NC, 2003), 27–28.

5. Steven Deyle, "The Domestic Slave Trade in America: The Lifeblood of the Southern Slave System," in Walter Johnson, ed., *The Chattel Principle: Internal Slave Trades in the Americas* (New Haven, CT, 2004), 95.

6. Ibid.

7. S. F. Hale to B. Magoffin, Governor of the Commonwealth of

Kentucky, Dec. 27, 1860, quoted in C. B. Dew, *Apostles of Disunion,* 92–93.

8. Journal of the [Mississippi] State Convention (Jackson, MS, 1861), 87–88.

9. Quoted in Bancroft, *Slave Trading in the Old South,* 116.

10. Philip J. Schwarz, "Hector Davis (1816–1863)," www.virginiamemory .com. This biographical entry is scheduled for publication in vol. 4 of John T. Kneebone et al., eds., *Dictionary of Virginia Biography* (3 vols. to date, Richmond, 1998–). See also Maurie D. McInnis, *Slaves Waiting for Sale: Abolitionist Art and the American Slave Trade* (Chicago, 2011), 103, 115–16.

11. Advertisement in J. W. Randolph, *Richmond Business Directory for 1858–59* (Richmond, VA, 1858), 54.

12. "Chap. 112.—An Act to incorporate the Traders Bank in the City of Richmond. Passed February 18, 1860," *Acts of the General Assembly of the State of Virginia Passed in 1859–60* (Richmond, VA, 1860), 15–16; Schwarz, "Hector Davis."

13. Hector Davis & Co., Slave Sales Record Book, 1857–1865, 2 vols., CHM. My thanks particularly to Debbie Vaughn of the CHM Library staff for making these manuscript volumes available to me.

14. Hector Davis & Co., Slave Sales Record Book, 1860–65, p. 84, CHM.

15. David W. Blight, *A Slave No More: Two Men Who Escaped to Freedom, Including Their Own Narratives of Emancipation* (Orlando, FL, 2007), 58.

16. Betts & Gregory, Auctioneers, Richmond, VA, Slave Price Circular, July 20, 1860, reproduced in Tadman, *Speculators and Slaves,* 58.

17. Dickinson, Hill & Co. to "Dear Sir," Aug. 25, 1860, William A. J. Finney Papers, DU.

18. Betts & Gregory to "Dear Sir," Aug. 28, 1860, ibid.

19. Betts & Gregory to "Dear Sir," Nov. 9, 1860, ibid.

20. Dickinson, Hill & Co., Dec. 28, 1860, photostat of original broadside, in Ray O. Hummel, Southeastern Broadsides, 1702–1982, State Government Records Collection, Library of Virginia, Richmond, VA.

21. V. O. Witcher to Betts & Gregory, Feb. 22, 1861, Cornelius Chase

Family Papers, LC. Following quotations from letters to Betts & Gregory are from this same source.

22. W. H. Betts to "Dear Jack," Feb. 20, 1861, ibid.

23. *Richmond Enquirer,* April 18–20, 1861; Bancroft, *Slave Trading in the Old South,* 103.

24. S. McD. Moore to J. D. Davidson, March 29, 1861, James D. Davidson Papers, McCormick Collection, SHSW.

25. Moore to Davidson, April 6, 1861, ibid.

26. Bill of Sale signed by R. H. Davis, Richmond, VA, Jan. 7, 1865, Slavery in the U.S. Collection, AAS.

IN CONCLUSION

1. W. H. Betts to "Dear Jack," Feb. 20 1861, Cornelius Chase Family Papers, LC.

2. W. H. Betts to W. H. Macfarland, Feb. 20, 1861, ibid.

3. Joseph Pointer to R. H. Dickinson, Feb. 10, 1846, Slavery in the U.S. Collection, AAS.

4. Dickinson, Hill & Co. to "Dear Sir," Dec. 20, 1858, Joseph Dickinson Papers, DU.

5. W. S. Mallicote to Betts & Gregory, Feb. 22, 1861, Cornelius Chase Family Papers, LC.

6. T. H. Lipscomb to Browning, Moore & Co., July 31, 1860, ibid.

7. P. N. Dulin to Betts & Gregory, May 25, 1861, Slavery in the U.S. Collection, AAS.

8. J. O. Stanfield to Browning, Moore & Co., Feb. 15, 186[0], Cornelius Chase Family Papers, LC.

9. Ann O. Davis to William W. Davis, Feb. 4, 1858, Jordan & Davis Papers, McCormick Collection, SHSW.

10. *Lynchburg Virginian,* Dec. 18, 1826.

11. P. H. Leuba to Thomas J. Randolph, Jan. 11, 1827, Thomas J. Randolph Papers, UVA.

12. Eavans McCrery to Elizabeth McCrery, Jan. [8], 1854, Anderson Family Papers, UVA.

INDEX

Page numbers in italics indicate illustrations.